International Relations at LSE
A History of 75 Years

International Relations at LSE

A History of 75 Years

Edited by
Harry Bauer
Elisabetta Brighi

Millennium Publishing Group
London School of Economics
London

First published 2003 by the
MILLENNIUM PUBLISHING GROUP
London School of Economics and Political Science,
Houghton Street, London WC2A 2AE
United Kingdom
http://www.e-millennium.ac

British Library Cataloguing in Publication Data.
A catalogue record of this book is available
from the British Library.

ISBN 0-9544397-0-8

Typeset by Millennium Publishing Group, London
Printed and bound in Great Britain by
Antony Rowe Ltd, Chippenham, Wiltshire

Contents

Contents

Notes on Contributors

James Der Derian is Professor of Political Science at the University of Massachusetts at Amherst and Professor of International Relations (Research) at Brown University where he directs the InfoTechWarPeace Project, *www.infopeace.org*. He was awarded a Rhodes Scholarship to study at Oxford University, where he completed a MPhil and DPhil in International Relations under the supervision of Hedley Bull.

Hugh Dyer is Senior Lecturer in International Studies at the University of Leeds. He was co-editor of Volume 16 of *Millennium: Journal of International Studies*. Some years ago Philip Windsor was an examiner of his PhD, taken at the LSE.

Mark Hoffman is Lecturer in the Department of International Relations, LSE and Dean of Undergraduate Studies. He was co-editor of Volume 10 of *Millennium: Journal of International Studies,* served as Associate Editor on Volumes 11-13, and is now a member of the Journal's Board of Trustees.

James Mayall is Professor Emeritus of International Relations at the LSE. He taught in the Department between 1966 and 1998 and was Convenor between 1991 and 1994. In 1998 he was appointed as the first Sir Patrick Sheehy Professor of International Relations in the University of Cambridge. He was elected a Fellow of the British Academy in 2001.

Roger Morgan was Lecturer at Aberystwyth between 1959 and 1963, and at Sussex between 1963 and 1967, under Martin Wight. He later worked at Chatham House, Loughborough University, the Policy Studies Institute, and the European University Institute, Florence. He has given occasional lectures at the School since the 1960s, and is currently Visiting Examiner for the LSE External Study programme.

F.S. Northedge (1918-1985) was Lecturer, Reader and Professor in the Department of International Relations at LSE between 1949 and 1984 and served as Convenor of the Department between 1969 and 1972. A prolific writer in the fields of international institutions and foreign policy, in 1971 he founded the student-run journal *Millennium: Journal of International Studies.*

Ronen Palan earned his Undergraduate and PhD degrees at the Department of International Relations, LSE. He currently teaches at the University of Sussex. Publications include: *The Offshore World,* 2003; *The Imagined Economies of Globalisation,* 2004 (with Angus Cameron); and *State Strategies in the Global Political Economy,* 1996 (with Jason Abbott).

Brian Porter studied International Relations at LSE between 1951 and 1961. On staff of Universities of Khartoum, Aberystwyth and now Kent. He is Fellow of the Royal Historical Society and, among other publications, has edited Martin Wight's *International Theory: The Three Traditions* with Gabriele Wight.

Martin Wight (1913-1972) was Lecturer and Reader in the Department of International Relations, LSE between 1949 and 1961. He became Professor of Modern History and the first Dean of the School of European Studies at the University of Sussex between 1961 and 1972. Works such as *Systems of States, Power Politics,* and *International Theory: The Three Traditions* have had a world-wide and lasting impact on the study of international politics.

Preface

The idea to publish a book on the 75 Years of
International Relations at the LSE took shape in our first
weeks as *Millennium* editors, in the winter of 2001. At that
time, it seemed to us a rather innocent one—but in
retrospect, we should have known better. The journey
which led us through the last three quarters of a century
in and around this institution was a fascinating one, but it
was by no means devoid of surprises and paradoxes.

A number of them stood out as soon as we became
serious about the project. Firstly, a volume that aspired,
as ours did, to sketch experiences, recollections and
analyses from no less than 75 years, and in such a
complex academic environment as the LSE, was
undoubtedly a highly sensitive and ambitious one.
Combined with our limited editorial experience, this
should have been enough of a deterrent for us both; but
naturally, it wasn't. Secondly, it was somewhat ironic (if
not infuriating, for some) that the idea for such a volume
would not come from the Department itself, but from two
Editors of *Millennium*—a journal which, as many in this
volume recall, has probably been the most successful yet
most intractable alien to occupy the Department's
premises.

Yet, these and other paradoxes, more than our own
perseverance, have kept the project prospering through

the several months of its creation. In our view, it is really such paradoxes and contradictions that offer a particularly apt, if not the best, angle to approach the present collection of essays.

Far from representing the last word on the subject, the contributions that follow merely offer a point of departure to investigate an articulate history which we have found to have many protagonists, a rather complex plot, and a number of equally fascinating counter-plots. As the subtitle to the book makes clear, this is in other words *a* history—and by no means *the* history of 75 Years of IR at LSE.

Thus, just as the latest intellectual fashion has it, the silences of this book are probably as important as its expressions—not least in such a plural, though not necessarily pluralistic, Department as this one. There are still many narratives to be told and myths to be called into question, all of which should have deserved equal attention in the pages of this book: the trajectory of radical thinking inside the Department; a critical evaluation of one of its founding figures, Charles Manning, and his legacy; the role of women; the relations between this Department and other Departments inside and outside LSE; and finally, a 'view from below', i.e., how the Department has been seen by its students.

The book, as the reader will no doubt realise, is more an experiment than a definitive statement, an *incipit* more than a conclusion, an invitation for dialogue, rather than an impersonal account of its achievements. Its character is also particularly hybrid and inconsistent: it ranges from the anecdotal to the theoretical, from the historical to the analytical, in order to evoke, reflect and assess.

In its opening part, the volume offers for the first time—yet, we are certain, not for the last—a 'story' of the 'departmental history'. However, resembling the famous mountain in that infamous jibe, this history could be pictured in countless ways—those represented here will not go uncontested, nor would everyone subscribe to them, but they certainly are original.

Without attempting to be exhaustive, the second part of the book presents a taste of the main intellectual forces that have driven the Department: from Martin Wight to Hedley Bull, from Philip Windsor and Susan Strange to *Millennium*. Beside a critical examination of their contributions, this part evokes images of quintessential academic experiences such as the idea of research as an intellectual journey, the tension between innovation and tradition, and the exciting and contradictory relation between students and mentors. This should be enough, we believe, to invite sustained reflection on the direction that the Department has followed in its first 75 years, and will continue to follow in the future.

All this would not have been possible without support and advice from inside and outside the Department. Most of all, our authors were, despite other academic and personal commitments, very willing to participate in this project. Without their generosity this book would not have come into existence. We also have to thank Gabriele Wight and the children of the late F.S. Northedge, Tilly, Chris and Alaistair, for their kind permission to publish pieces posthumously.

One of the most joyful moments of working on this book was to experience a community of alumni, former and recent staff members and former editors of *Millennium* who all cared about this project; this more than repaid us for those rare episodes of resistance and reluctance which we encountered while busy with this project. Michael Banks, Chris Brown, Barry Buzan, Michael Donelan, Stefano Guzzini, Carsten Holbraad, Geoffrey Stern, and Peter Wilson have all given us indispensable advice and feedback on earlier parts of this book. Martina Langer swiftly and reliably helped us with the preparation of some manuscripts, while Hilary Parker has proved an indispensable source of advice and help with contacts. Margot Light, Convenor of the

Department, has patiently and generously offered us her unfailing support from the beginning of the enterprise. Miriam Rycroft and Rashmi Singh, both as *Millennium* business managers, have helped with administrative work throughout while the current editors, Eva Gross and Alvaro Méndez, readily cooperated with us. Catherine Mo and Nisha Shah have cheered us up and dealt with editorial work in what turned out to be the very beginning of this enterprise. Scott Harris was a great help during the same time. A very special word of thanks goes to Christopher Hill, who has always been available and has never been too tired to listen and advise us for the better. Finally, just to end with one more paradox, we would like to dedicate this book to its editors, who only know about the many more paradoxes that this book contains.

HB & EB

Foreword

James Mayall

It is a privilege and a pleasure to have been asked to contribute the Foreword to this volume of essays that *Millennium* is publishing in commemoration of the 75th anniversary of the LSE Department of International Relations. Everyone who is concerned with the School—and with the place of our subject within it—will be profoundly grateful to the editors. From its foundation at the end of the 19th century, the LSE played the pivotal role in the development of the social sciences in Britain, and as a result of its international reputation, across much of the rest of the world as well. Readers of Lord Dahrendorf's otherwise admirable centenary history would have to conclude, however, that International Relations (IR) had only the smallest of walk on parts in this triumphal saga. How is this account to be squared with the Department's current prominence in the School's affairs and, as Brian Porter points out in his contribution to this volume, its occupation of the prime site in the School? This book puts the record straight.

In part, the explanation for the Department's apparent invisibility in the School's early history is that the LSE has always meant different things to different people, even different social scientists. After thirty-two years in Houghton Street—getting on for half its existence—it seemed to me extraordinary that there was no consensus on the central role that the Department had played in establishing IR as an important area of social enquiry in its own right. Located in a school of social sciences, the Department was strategically placed to develop IR as an interdisciplinary subject and as a site for a vigorous internal debate about the underlying structure and day-to-day processes of world politics.

This is indeed more or less what happened, but its significance was not immediately apparent. I should not have been surprised. It is a strange fact about the LSE that its external reputation often bore little relation to what was going on inside. Soon after joining the Department—Paul Taylor and I joined on the same day in 1966, two years after Michael Donelan and one after Philip Windsor—I attended a meeting in Vienna with Michael and Philip. I can no longer remember what the organisation that ran the conference was called but it had been set up by people, many of whom were considered in the West to be fellow travellers, but who considered themselves to be gate-keepers of an earlier internationalism during a bleak period when academic communication across the iron curtain was strained close to breaking point.

Representatives of the LSE were sought after not so much because of their individual expertise but because the School itself was believed by the organisers to be ideologically acceptable. I remember two things about this conference. The first was the way that the beautifully dressed and ideologically inflexible Marxists from the University of Darmstadt terrified the apparatchiks from Eastern Europe; the second was an incident that occurred over lunch on the first day. 'Wasn't it a tragedy', an elderly and, I was told, eminent historian from East Berlin, confided 'what had happened to the LSE'. I was at some loss how to reply. From my point of view the LSE was far from a tragedy: it had just given me a job to do what I wanted to do and believed needed doing.

But it gradually became clear that his LSE was not mine. He regarded the succession of Harold Laski by Michael Oakeshott as a great betrayal, and he seemed to overlook altogether the fact that while Laski held sway over the study of Politics at the School, Lionel Robbins had made the LSE the bastion of neo-classical Economics against the Keynesian revolution—designed to save capitalism from itself and orchestrated not from the radical LSE but from Establishment Cambridge. Even less would he have recognised the LSE of Charles Manning, Geoffrey Goodwin, Fred Northedge, Martin Wight and Hedley Bull, who despite their differences, had grasped the essential point that in an increasingly integrated world, international relations were too important for their study to be left to the historians, lawyers and economists, each charting their own course, and for the most part sailing past one another like ships in the night.

What is remarkable about the LSE as an institution is not its identification with a particular set of political beliefs, but that from the beginning it has insisted that the Academy should be a part of the world it studies, not something rarified or removed from it. Whether the creation of the discipline of IR has been wholly successful in this respect is still a disputed question. Nor was this creation the work of the LSE alone. The first professorship in IR was established in Aberystwyth several years before Charles Manning took up his post as the first Montague Burton Professor at the LSE. Ever since, the two departments have engaged in a kind of anthropological joking relationship in which they contest the strategic role the other has played in the progressive professionalisation of the subject. But, if only because of its location and the impact of its graduates on the staffing of IR and Politics departments in this country and further afield, it is not just tribal loyalty that persuades me that had the LSE not existed, it is unlikely that the effort would ever have been made.

The LSE did not have formal departments until the 1960s and not everyone would accept the subsequent fragmentation of the social sciences as an unmixed blessing. As Susan Strange was to discover when she pioneered research and teaching in International Political Economy, attacking the arbitrary disciplinary boundaries with which the economists had encircled themselves was likely to lead to the erection of new and equally inconvenient ones: in this case those erected by the IR scholars themselves as they attempted to professionalise the subject and fight off interlopers. Nonetheless, if the subject was ever to take its place self-confidently in cross as well as intra-disciplinary debates, as its practitioners increasingly do, it was probably both necessary and inevitable that the effort should be made.

The essays in this volume provide a fascinating insight into this effort—its successes and its failures. If there was a 'project' to develop a discipline, some of the successes, such as the extraordinary influence of Philip Windsor during the 1970s and 1980s, to which Hugh Dyer rightly draws attention, were not intended to have this result. Dahrendorf implied that by preferring the traditional and philosophical approach to the study of IR, the LSE had somehow missed the behavioural tide that was flowing so strongly across the Atlantic during the 1970s. So it did, but from the perspective of the early 21st century, quite rightly so. There can be little doubt that it is the debate between realists, rationalist and revolutionists, of whatever kind, but always near the centre of IR at the LSE, that provides the more interesting but also more useful starting point from which to map the confusing post Cold-War political landscape.

It is of course no more than a starting point, its utility very often being its capacity to act as a creative irritant on those who are more impressed by its shortcomings than its merits. Michael Donelan added to these famous categories, fideism and natural law and one has only to read the recent report of the International Commission on

Intervention and State Sovereignty *The Responsibility to Protect* to detect the resurgence of his influence and those who shared his belief in the just war tradition. Although the tradition of contrasting world views was always deeply rooted in the Department, its members were never committed as a group to a single orthodoxy. Indeed, the irritant often energised those within the Department, such as Philip Windsor himself and two more recent recruits, Chris Brown and Barry Buzan, to move beyond its traditional categories.

A synthetic subject, whose boundaries cannot easily be fixed by functional or reductionist criteria, will always be vulnerable to attacks from the more sharply focused disciplines on which it draws. There is simply no methodology on which all IR specialists can agree, as economists can, even when on matters of substance they stand on opposite sides of the barricades. It will also, one suspects, be more than usually susceptible to all those who periodically try to sell the Emperor a suit of new clothes. This is why the development of a core IR curriculum, to which Geoffrey Goodwin devoted his energy, was so important. Indeed, the influence of the LSE IR curriculum is still felt almost anywhere that IR is taught as an academic subject. Within the Department it provided at least the illusion of a solid ground on which to stand. Deep down many of us may have suspected that the anti-foundationalists had a point, but the need to ground our teaching in the History of International Politics, Institutions and Foreign Policy Analysis was itself some protection against the temptation to make the subject into a kind of meta-social science whose pretensions and ambitions were so great that they could never conceivably be realised.

Curricula are not exciting in themselves but they create the architectural framework within which exciting things can happen. Intellectual excitement is what an LSE education is all about. Two final comments will give the flavour of the Department's contribution to this brew.

The first, as I have already suggested, is that while many of those who are identified with the 'English School' taught in the Department at some point in their careers, it was never captured by one methodological or philosophical position. As well as those such as Geoffrey Stern and myself, who might be loosely classified as belonging to the English School, the Department embraced those who were impatient with English School classicism such as Michael Banks, a whole raft of regional and foreign policy specialists such as Christopher Hill, Michael Leifer, Michael Yahuda, and Margot Light, students of revolution and political sociology like Fred Halliday and Justin Rosenberg, and an anarchic and marvellously idiosyncratic realist such as Christopher Coker. Those who have joined the Department more recently are similarly spread along the intellectual spectrum. The fact that the curriculum has always been sufficiently elastic to allow for this kind of pluralism makes it a particularly congenial place to work.

My final comment appropriately concerns *Millennium*. Because the Department has always encouraged debate, it provided the environment in which *Millennium* could not only grow to be one of the leading professional journals in the field, and a role model for many later graduate run journals on both sides of the Atlantic. Paradoxically, despite its apparently conservative structure, it was also an environment which, as Mark Hoffman recalls, the Journal could frequently run ahead of by challenging the mainstream positions favoured within it. It is not fanciful, I believe, to see this volume as a fitting tribute to the dynamic but mutually beneficial tension between these two partners.

The Department of International Relations at LSE
A Brief History, 1924–1971[*]

F.S. Northedge

The First World War may be regarded as having been the starting point of the university study in the United Kingdom of International Relations (IR) or International Politics; the two expressions have all along been generally regarded as synonymous. That conflict, the scale of which was foreseen by scarcely anyone in 1914, seemed to have demonstrated the need for some special study of the modern society of states and the wider diffusion of knowledge of that society, if such catastrophes were to be avoided in the future. It is sobering, however, to note that the first provision for teaching and research in international studies was initiated, not through action by any university authorities, but through the generosity of a private benefactor. It was the late Lord Davies of Llandinam, an industrialist and former Liberal M.P., who founded the first Chair of International Politics at the University College of Wales, Aberystwyth in 1919.

[*] We would like to thank Tilly, Alastair and Chris Northedge for their generous permission to publish this piece. We are also indebted to Christopher Hill for his help in excavating it.

At the LSE itself international studies in the immediate
aftermath of the First World War were represented solely
by the teaching of Public International Law, a subject
with which IR was soon to be intimately associated. This
legal teaching was at first provided by A. Pearce Higgins,
who held at one and the same time the Chair of
International Law in the University of London and the
Whewell Chair of International Law in the University of
Cambridge; among his courses at the LSE in the session
1922-23 was one entitled 'Some treaties since 1915
affecting International Relations', which appears to have
been the first, albeit oblique, reference to IR in the
School's teaching programme. In the following session
Pearce Higgins lectured also on 'The League of Nations at
Work', so initiating that study of international institutions
which has always since then formed an integral part of
the International Relations Department's province. In his
general international law teaching Pearce Higgins was
assisted by Arnold D. McNair—later Lord McNair and
member successively of the Permanent Court of
International Justice and the International Court of Justice
at The Hague. In that same session (1923-24), too, A.E.
Zimmern, first Professor of International Politics at
Aberystwyth and subsequently Montague Burton
Professor of IR at Oxford, did some teaching at the
School, though this was under the heading of Political
Science.

The real breakthrough for IR came, however, in 1924,
when—for five years only in the first instance and then
only on a part-time basis—a Chair in IR was instituted.
This was provided for by the trustees of the Sir Ernest
Cassell Fund, the Chair being at that stage given the
Cassell name, after a benefactor to whose munificence the
School was beholden for the financing of posts in other
fields as well. The first to hold the Chair was Philip Noel-
Baker, then a Fellow of King's College, Cambridge, who
had gained international experience at the Paris Peace

Conference in 1919 as secretary to Lord Robert Cecil, afterwards Lord Cecil of Chelwood. (Cecil was Chairman at Noel-Baker's Inaugural Lecture on 'The Study of International Relations', given at the School on 7 October 1924.) Noel-Baker held the Chair until 1929 when leaving academic life, he became Labour M.P. for Coventry and Parliamentary Private Secretary to Arthur Henderson, the Foreign Secretary in the second Labour Government. After the Second World War Noel-Baker was to hold a number of posts in Labour Governments and in 1959 he won the Nobel Peace Prize for his work for disarmament, work which may be considered to have begun, so far as his published writings were concerned, with his study *Disarmament*, which first appeared in 1926, during his period of teaching at the School.

Noel-Baker's primary interests as a professor included the study of the peaceful settlement of international disputes—his book *The Geneva Protocol*, dealing with that most famous abortive project, was published in 1925—and the international position of the self-governing Dominions, as they then were called. From his teaching on this latter subject sprang his authoritative work *The Present Juridical Status of the British Dominions in International Law*, published in 1929.[1] Noel-Baker's work at the School was so successful that Sir William Beveridge, the then Director, in his annual report on the session 1925-26, referred to the creation of the Chair as having been of the greatest value, and announced that the School's staff in the field of international studies was to be augmented by the assignment to it by the Senate of the University of a Chair of International History founded by Sir Daniel Stevenson. 'The School', the Director went on, 'will thus be equipped to deal with international affairs from all the three angles of law, history and administration'. The last of these three 'angles' presumably reflected the general assumption in the 1920s that an international community of states already existed: what remained to be accomplished being to furnish that community with appropriate administrative organs, the most important of which had already been set up in the form of the League of Nations. The first incumbent of the Stevenson Chair (later to be called the Stevenson Research Chair in International History and to be assigned to the Royal Institute of International Affairs) was Arnold J. Toynbee, who inaugurated his tenure of it by giving three public lectures at the School on 'Aspects of International History Since the War'.

The next step forward came in 1927, when a grant from the Laura Spelman Rockefeller Memorial Fund made it possible to gather the work being variously done at LSE for the study of international problems into a distinct Department of International Studies 'having a unity of its own, though closely in touch with all the rest of the work in the School'. Consistently with the chronic dependence of academic studies at the School on building developments, the full implementation of this new departure, the Director stated, 'must wait until the new building in Houghton Street' (that is, the present-day main entrance and the building along the west side of Houghton Street) 'and once the roof is completed'. But the decision had already been made for the establishment of a full-time Chair of International Law, for the appointment of two or more teachers in the field of international problems, for the issue of an *Annual Digest of Public International Law Cases*,[2] and for the formulation of a 'comprehensive course of international studies'.

Included in the new staff were famous names: S.H. Bailey, from Sidney Sussex College, Cambridge, who was to die at thirty-four in 1938, Lucy B. Mair, later Professor Mair, from Newnham College, Cambridge, and Hersch (later Sir Hersch) Lauterpacht all began their academic careers as lecturers or assistant lecturers in International Studies as a consequence of the new development. As part-time teacher, Sir Anton Bertram, an ex-Chief Justice of Ceylon, gave lectures on 'The Government of the

British Empire outside the Dominions and their Dependencies', and H.A. Grimshaw, after whom is named the now long-established staff-student club of the IR Department, who was then Chief of the Native Labour Section of the International Labour Office (ILO), gave a course of lectures on the working of that organisation.

S.H. Bailey's teaching was principally on the economic aspects of international relations. Miss Mair assisted the Professor generally, while Lauterpacht, consistently with his later fame, brought new vigour to the teaching of the legal aspects of relations between states. It is noteworthy how, already at this early stage in the development of IR at the School, so many specialists from cognate disciplines were being called upon to contribute their learning to the expanding provision for international studies. Thus, A. Meyendorff, then a Reader in the University in Russian Institutions and Economics, lectured on 'Cultural Contacts between the West and Other Civilisations', while it was likewise under the rubric of international studies that those eminent anthropologists, or ethnologists as they were then called, Professors Seligman and Malinowski, assisted by J.H. Driberg, taught a course entitled 'Cultural Contacts between the West and Primitive Peoples'. It was Noel-Baker, however, who continued to shoulder the main burden of that teaching which might be described as the 'core' for 'all these loosely affiliated subjects', the teaching, namely, of IR, defined by him as a 'general survey of the nature of relations between the governments and peoples of different countries'.

Already in those days papers on special aspects of international studies could be taken in the Finals examination of the B.Sc. (Economics), but it was not until 1930 that IR as a special subject in Finals made its appearance in the University regulations, and even so still in conjunction, as a twin special subject , with International Law. But before dealing with developments in and after 1930, when the occupancy of the Chair of IR was to change, it is worth summarising the state of international studies, as the subject or complex of subjects continued to be called, at the end of the 1920s.

Noel-Baker, taking as his particular purview the 'Political Aspects of the Society of States', 'International Relations', and 'International Institutions and the Inter-Imperial Relations of the British Empire', had the assistance of Miss Mair and S.H. Bailey respectively in seminars on 'Pacific Methods of Settling International Disputes' and on 'Economic Aspects of International Relations', and in the treatment of 'Current International Events'. On their own accounts, Miss Mair lectured on 'Problems of Colonial Government' and on the 'Protection of Minorities', and S.H. Bailey on the ILO, replacing Harold Grimshaw in this respect, on 'International Technical Government', which comprised 'an examination of the development, organisation and work of international associations and bureaux in the Nineteenth and Twentieth Centuries', and on the 'Machinery of Diplomacy'. On the legal side, H.A. Smith, formerly Professor of Constitutional Law at McGill University, who had been appointed to the newly created Chair of International Law at the School, gave his Inaugural Lecture on 'The Diplomatic Unity of the Empire' in October 1928, while Dr. Lauterpacht discoursed throughout the session on the 'History of International Arbitration', and on the 'Work of the Permanent Court of International Justice'. Dr. Meyendorff, Professors Seligman and Malinowski, assisted by Miss Mair and Mr. (later Professor) Schapera, continued their work on the cultural aspects of international relations, while Sir Anton Bertram continued with his teaching on 'Government in the British Empire outside the Dominions and their Dependencies'.

This many-sidedness as a branch of university study has continued to mark the subject of IR until the present day. Moreover, anticipations of still further developments were provided by a course of lectures on 'Disarmament' delivered in 1928 by that internationally acknowledged authority on international relations, Don Salvador de Madariaga, and by a further course on the geographical aspects of current international problems. Indeed, one might say, then and now, that there is and always has been scarcely a department within the LSE which has not had its contribution to make to the study of IR, though without of course affecting the primacy of its central intellectual core.

Two developments of about this time are worth a passing mention. First, the introduction in 1927 of the course for a diploma in Diplomatic Studies, described as specially adapted for students either seeking posts in the diplomatic or consular services or already holding such posts. For this, in 1930, there was substituted the course leading in appropriate cases to the award of a Certificate in International Studies. This was in principle of two years' duration, but in exceptional instances could be taken in one year. The examination comprised six papers covering the main branches of IR and including one paper opted for from a list of alternative possibilities. Those eligible to enter upon this course were now described as 'students of relatively advanced standing' (though they need not necessarily be graduates) 'who wish to devote their whole time to subjects within the general field of International Relations'. This Certificate course, while meeting always a limited need, lasted until the 1960s, when it was discontinued with the advent of the new one-year M.Sc. in the Faculty of Economics with IR as one of its branches.

The other development came in March 1929 when the School joined with the Royal Institute of International Affairs (RIIA) in entertaining in London a conference, the second of many to be summoned annually by the League Committee for Intellectual Co-operation, of 'institutions for the scientific study of International Relations'. This was but one—and early—example of the half-century of close relations between the School and Chatham House (the RIIA), a co-operation symbolised and administered by the so-called British Co-ordinating Committee for International Studies, on which the Director and members of the IR Department represented the School and the Director-General and other officials the Institute. The Committee, first formed in 1930 and designed to serve as a centre of communication with comparable committees abroad, now includes representatives of many universities and other eligible institutions throughout the land.

In catering for the School's participation in the International Studies Conference, the Department played throughout an important role. It was in this same context that S.H. Bailey initiated that series of conferences of United Kingdom teachers which have come to bear his name. Following the demise of the League of Nations, the International Studies Conference fell into abeyance soon after the War. Nothing has replaced it since.

A new era for IR at the School had begun in January 1930 when, on a full-time basis, C.A.W. Manning succeeded Noel-Baker in the Sir Ernest Cassell Chair, which he held—though later, as will presently be explained, under a different designation—until his retirement in 1962. Manning, who had served successively in the ILO and the League Secretariat in Geneva, had since been a Fellow and Tutor in Law at New College, Oxford. His legal background, as with Noel-Baker, enabled him to act as a bridge between the two closely associated subjects, IR and International Law, at the School. Always with a more evident commitment to the development of the first degree teaching subject than to the demands of research—his most significant work, reflecting his matured thinking on his subject, *The Nature of International Society*,[3] was published in 1962—he included among his agenda interests the establishing of the subject's distinctive place in the training of the young for life in the modern world, the sharpening of his pupils' mental powers by what some might wish to term the Socratic method, as opposed to the mere imparting of knowledge, and the assertion and demonstration of the relevance of a range of social disciplines, from Economics to Psychology, to the study of the behaviour of states in the international society. Manning, who had inherited from Noel-Baker his staple courses on 'International Relations', on 'International Institutions', and on the 'External Relations of the Dominions', along with the seminar on 'Current Events', was never backward in acknowledging the assistance afforded him in his early professorial years by S.H. Bailey on the 'Economic Aspects of International Relations', by Lucy Mair on the 'Pacific Settlement of International Disputes', and by the late L.G. Robinson, from 1930 a Reader in International History and later the School's Dean of Postgraduate Studies. Robinson lectured in the 1930s on the 'Geographical Background of International Relations' and on 'European Diplomacy from 1870 to 1919'.

In 1932 the Department was weakened by the absence of Miss Mair for a year of anthropological fieldwork in East Africa with a Rockefeller Fellowship. After returning she was gradually to transfer to Colonial Administration: this partly in connection with a course then recently organised under the general charge of J. Coatman, Professor of Imperial Economic Relations.

Meanwhile, however, the scene was considerably enlivened by the arrival, after a tenure of the Chair of International Politics at Aberystwyth, of the exhilarating personality of C.K. (later Sir Charles) Webster as Stevenson Professor of International History, Toynbee now making the RIIA his permanent home as Stevenson Research Professor of International History. Webster, who had already achieved renown as an adviser to the British delegation at the Paris Peace Conference in 1919 and by his major studies of Castlereagh and the Congress of Vienna in 1815, at first supplemented L.G. Robinson's diplomatic history teaching by covering the period from 1815 to 1848 for IR specialists in his characteristically vigorous style. He also contributed to the Department's work by lecturing on 'British Foreign Policy in the 19th and 20th Centuries', thus anticipating the course on 'British Foreign Policy' to be given in the late 1950s by F.S. Northedge, which paved the way to the teaching in the Department of the 'Foreign Policies of the Great Powers'.

Thus the 1930s slipped by. A blow fell in 1934 when the Sir Ernest Cassell Trustees announced that they could not renew their grant to support the Chair of IR at the School; their original grant in 1924 had already been extended once beyond its initial five-year term. Anxiety was, however, relieved when in 1936 Sir Montague Burton agreed to make a gift for the partial endowment of the Chair, the name of which was accordingly changed. In those years, too, the deteriorating international situation was reflected by lectures given in the Department in 1936 on 'Belgium and the Balance of Power' by Dr. Emile Cammaerts, Professor of Belgian Studies and Institutions in the University of London, and in 1937 by a lecture series in the IR Department on 'Peaceful Change'—the lectures, assembled and edited by Manning,[4] being then published as a volume under that same title—and by lectures on the life and death of the Weimar Republic in Germany given in the Summer Term of 1938 by Dr. A.M. Wagner, a lecturer in German at the School. That year also saw the Department's loss, by untimely death, of S.H. Bailey, whose teaching in the field of international technical co-operation was, but for the coming of war, to have been carried on by Dr. F. Chalmers Wright, a former President of the Students' Union, who was however to leave the Department for an important post with the United Nations in 1947.

During the Second World War, when the School was accommodated in Peterhouse, Cambridge, the staff of the Department was, like that of so many other departments, severely depleted. Manning himself having gone off to work with wartime Chatham House under the Foreign Office, and Chalmers Wright to more dangerous adventures, L.G. Robinson, busy Dean though he remained of Postgraduate Studies, was left to teach 'International Relations', as well as 'European Diplomacy from 1871 to 1919' and the 'Geographical Background to International Relations', albeit with notable assistance from Dr. (now Professor) Georg Schwarzenberger of University College, London, who lectured on the 'Pacific Methods of Settling International Disputes'. In time, however, for the session 1943-44 Manning, rejoining the School at Cambridge, resumed there his lecturing on 'International Relations'.

It was at this stage that the Department's Special Subject in the final two years of the B.Sc. (Economics) degree became IR only, the associated subject International Law being dropped from its title, though it was to remain a required subject for IR specialists for a further twenty-seven years.

With the coming of peace in 1945 and the return of the School to its London home, the stage was set for a restoration and gradual expansion of the Department as men and women back from the war flooded into Houghton Street, almost all with lives affected, and perhaps embittered, by the collapse of the international system in the 1930s, and many with appetites resultingly whetted for the serious study of this and other momentous occurrences in the common life of nations. The first of the new intake of recruits to the Department's teaching staff was the late W.C.B. Tunstall, appointed in 1946 to lecture on 'International History Between the Two Wars', on 'the Strategic Aspects of International Politics' (author of many books on the British navy and naval warfare, he had been a naval correspondent for the BBC during the war), as well as on S.H. Bailey's old subject, the 'Machinery of Diplomacy'. With Chalmers-Wright dealing for a brief while with 'International Social and Economic Co-operation', and with Webster and Robinson covering the 'Diplomatic History of the Great Powers since 1815', Manning now resumed the bulk of his pre-war teaching programme. (Colonel Stephen Longrigg was one of several who helped out with short courses at this time.) The pre-war weekly discussions of current international issues were in particular now revived, the emphasis being not so much on a teaching of current history as on an exchange of reflections on the current functioning of the international system, this latter being seen as the prime concern for the IR specialist.

Next, in 1947, Frank Chambers—who, still in his fifties, was to die in harness in 1964—joined the Department to teach and supervise research in the domestic aspects of international affairs, this becoming an optional subject for IR specialists when the scheme for the B.Sc. (Economics) degree was revised in time for the Michaelmas Term, 1949. Chambers had already established his reputation with the publication of his *The War Behind The War*, a thorough and original study of political developments within the belligerent countries during the First World War. During his years in the Department—he was a Senior Lecturer at the time of his death—his literary output was impressive, including contributions to philosophy; his *This Age of Conflict*, first published in 1945 and written in conjunction with two other authors, has become a standard work in modern world history covering the years from 1914 until after the Second World War.[5]

At the beginning of 1948, Geoffrey Goodwin, himself a former student in the Department, returning from two years with the Foreign Office, succeeded Chalmers-Wright in the field of international social and economic co-operation. Goodwin later extended his scope from functional international organisations to the study of all-purpose international institutions such as the League and the United Nations and in recent years to European Institutions and European integration, together with the theory of IR embracing the study of both classical and contemporary writers in the field. His most notable work to date, *Britain and the United Nations*, was published in 1957 in the form of a report of a Chatham House study group under the auspices of the Carnegie Endowment for International Peace.[6] Appointed a Reader in 1958, he was to succeed Manning in 1962 as Montague Burton Professor of IR. It was principally through Goodwin's energy and enterprise that a Centre for International Studies (CIS) was set up in 1967 to encourage multi-disciplinary study and research, the main stress being in the first instance on the Soviet Union, Eastern Europe, Communist China, and their relations with the rest of the world. The Centre remains an integral part of the School, and closely linked with the IR Department, with many of the Fellows and Students of the Centre taking an active part in the work of the Department. The Centre was in the first instance financed by means of an award from the Ford Foundation. Goodwin was responsible (later with Michael Banks's help) for a Foreign Service Course which for ten years from 1955 trained over sixty graduate students from overseas (mainly from the Commonwealth) for their countries' diplomatic services; many of whom now hold senior diplomatic appointments.

Apart from these developments, the most notable change in the Department in the early post-war years had occurred in 1949 when the B.Sc. (Economics) degree syllabus was revised. In place of the old one-year Intermediate course which had included no provision for IR, there now was instituted a two-year Part I course which included, among other optional subjects, the 'Structure of International Society', an elementary introduction to the IR field: on this, until his retirement in

1962, Manning gave the lectures every year. Instead of the old two-year Finals course there now appeared a one-year Part II course in which IR, as before, could be taken as a Special Subject, but now with a range of optional sub-specialisms in addition to the old basic subjects of IR, International Institutions and International History. This represented a major step forward for the Department, as it meant that new students entering upon the B.Sc. at the School could have an approach to IR on their academic agenda from the outset, thus ensuring a steady source from which eventual specialisers in the subject would be drawn. At 1971, after a second revision of the degree in 1959, some eighty to ninety students, representing about one-third of the Schools total intake of B.Sc. students every year, elected to study this option. Of these, numbers varying between thirty-five and forty-five elect each year to take IR in the Part II.

New also at this stage was Manning's course on the 'Philosophical Aspects of International Relations', on which he was, after his retirement, to continue to lecture part-time. He also ran a weekly discussion period for graduates on philosophical issues. As if to help cope with this increase in student numbers, two new teachers were appointed in the Department in 1949: R.J.M. Wight, an Oxford historian who came from a research post at Chatham House to a Readership in IR at the School, and F.S. Northedge, who having taken IR as a Special Subject under Manning, now became an assistant lecturer in the Department. Martin Wight had distinguished himself by one of the most incisive existing analyses of international relations, entitled *Power Politics*, published in 1946, and later added to his reputation by his powerful contributions to the Chatham House *Survey of International Affairs*, entitled *The World in March 1939*, published in 1952, and edited by Arnold J. Toynbee and Frank T. Ashton-Gwatkin.[7] He took over from Manning the teaching of 'International Institutions' with an emphasis upon the United Nations as a forum of international politics rather than a piece of intergovernmental machinery; he also introduced a deservedly popular course of his own entitled 'International Theory', in which he surveyed the writings on the international system of outstanding thinkers from Thucydides to Lenin and Hitler. In 1961 he accepted the Chair of Modern European History in the University of Sussex, where he also became Dean of European Studies.

Northedge, on the other hand, was assigned by Manning the formidable task of providing teaching on 'Psychological Factors in International Relations', a course which, first given in 1951, remains both a pioneering one of its kind and a stable element in the Department's teaching arrangements. He then developed parallel interests, including British foreign policy on which he has published two volumes, *British Foreign Policy*, covering the period 1945 to 1961, and *The Troubled Giant*, covering the period 1916 to 1939, published in 1962 and 1966 respectively;[8] and 'International Politics', the core of the Department's teaching work, which formed the principal part of his teaching in 1971 and is deservedly a very popular course for a wide range of students within the School.

In 1955 Northedge won one of the two Carnegie Endowment Prizes for research in problems of international organisation. The title of Reader was conferred on him in 1960 and that of Professor in 1968. He succeeded Goodwin as Convenor of the Department in 1969. In 1971, he published, as co-author, *International Disputes: The Political Aspects*, to be mentioned again later, and *A Hundred Years of International Relations*.[9]

After the appointment of these two, expansion of the teaching staff of the Department was somewhat speeded up, to keep pace with increasing student numbers, and especially of those reading for higher degrees. In particular, there followed the development of regional studies, corresponding with the geographical expansion of the international system as a whole after the Second World War. Geoffrey Stern, joining the staff in 1956, quickly built up a place for himself as an authority on International Communism and Soviet foreign policy; he is the author of *Fifty Years of Communism*, published in 1967.[10] Later, in 1964, came Peter Lyon, specialising in South-East Asia, after serving a term in the Politics Department in Leicester University; in 1969 he left the Department to take an appointment as Senior Lecturer and Secretary at the Institute of Commonwealth Studies in the University of London. Then in January 1965 Dr. Coral Bell, who took a Ph.D. in the Department and had previously served in the Australian Diplomatic Service and lectured both at Sydney and Manchester Universities, came as a specialist on the Far East with particular reference to Chinese domestic and foreign policies. But she also had an exceptionally wide spread of interests. Her principal work to date, *Negotiation From Strength*,[11] published in 1962 before she joined the Department, is in the field of American foreign policy and while teaching in the Department she has, in addition, worked up practically single-handedly the study of 'Crisis Management' in the conduct of international relations.

Mention should also be made among the Department's recently acquired regional specialists of James Mayall and Paul Taylor, both appointed Lecturers in 1966, the former an Africanist, assistant editor with special reference to African questions of the Chatham House *Survey of International Affairs* and author of *Africa: The Cold War and After*,[12] and the latter a student of European institutions and the process and nature of the closer integration of states. Also under the heading of regional authorities is Michael Leifer, specialising in South-East Asian Studies and the author of a book on Cambodia; he is the latest recruit to the Department's staff, having been appointed in 1969 and having, like Coral Bell, Peter Lyon and F.S.

Northedge, taken his Ph.D. as a student in the Department.

Meanwhile, a notable addition to the Department's teaching strength in the traditional field of international institutions had been Alan James, who joined the Department in 1957. Following a year as a Research Fellow in Columbia University in New York in 1958, he was to produce the authoritative work on United Nations activities in the peacekeeping field entitled *The Politics of Peacekeeping*, issued under the auspices of the Institute for Strategic Studies in 1969.[13] James also did outstanding work in teaching the 'Structure of International Society', the first-year course, after Manning and then Northedge had in turn relinquished this subject; and he also developed single-handedly a new subject, 'The Sociology of International Law' which, under, new regulations approved by the University in 1971, formed an alternative to International Law as a compulsory subject for IR specialists in the B.Sc. (Economics). It is interesting that, with the appointment of Alan James—he became a Reader by title in 1970—the number of those teachers in the Department who had taken their first degrees in IR at the School increased to six: the others of these being Michael Banks (to be mentioned later), Geoffrey Goodwin, Peter Lyon, F.S. Northedge and Geoffrey Stern.

The subject IR in London was growing in keeping with the world-wide developments in the discipline as it spread to other countries, especially the United States. In 1963 Michael Banks joined the Department after a year spent in taking an M.A. at Lehigh University in the United States, where he caught the enthusiasm for the study of IR as a science, rather than—as it had been traditionally taught in the School—one of the humanities; he is the Departments foremost exponent of contemporary theory of IR while at the same time acting as somewhat of a bridge with the more classical schools of thought. Strategic Studies, a world-wide development of the late 1950s and the 1960s, was represented by

Hedley Bull, a recruit of 1959, and a Reader from 1963, whose *The Control of the Arms Race*, published under the auspices of the Institute for Strategic Studies in 1964, has become an international classic.[14] Bull was also to serve for two years as the Director of the newly established Disarmament and Arms Control Unit of the Foreign Office; on returning to the School he continued the work of Martin Wight in the field of international theory, until leaving the Department in 1968 to take up the Chair of IR in the University of Canberra.

The successor to Bull in the strategic studies field was Philip Windsor, whose appointment dates from 1965 and who became a Reader in 1968; his publications in the field of strategic studies and also German and East European politics are too numerous to mention, even selectively. In his teaching of Strategic Studies, which soon grew one of the most popular options for IR specialists in Part II of the degree, Windsor was to be assisted by Adam Roberts, who, joining the Department in 1968, made his own a new aspect of the subject, the study of civilian resistance to foreign invasion, and by Nicholas Sims, appointed in the same year, who while also specialising in Conflict and Conflict Resolution Studies, assisted Northedge in the still flourishing class on current international issues.

Yet another dimension to IR was contributed by Michael Donelan, who joined the Department in 1964 after having been Sir John Dill Fellow at Princeton University. He made himself responsible for Foreign Policy Analysis, which was made a compulsory subject for all IR specialists, also teaching United States foreign policy and assisting with the training of students in the Politics of International Economic Relations. Donelan's most substantial work to date, besides his many articles on international economic relations, is *International Disputes: the Political Aspects*, written in conjunction with F.S. Northedge for the David Davies Institute of International Studies.[15]

It will be seen that the history of the Department, especially since 1945, has been one of continuous expansion as well in student numbers as in the strength of its teaching staff—standing as it does at the time of writing at thirteen—as also in the areas of the subject covered by undergraduate instruction and the supervision of research. The Department's teaching now covers practically all the recognised sub-specialisms within the general subject and is provided by a predominantly young and vigorous team of specialists more numerous than those dealing with the subject in any other British university and perhaps in any other higher institute of education in Europe. As these pages have shown, many distinguished men and women, with their own authoritative contributions to the subject, have taught in the Department, which is accepted as a model and an example wherever attention is paid to the academic handling of this difficult but challenging branch of study. A high proportion of teaching posts in IR, as well in Britain as throughout the world are at present occupied by the Department's alumni. There are no reasons why this growth in influence and diversity within this single intellectual discipline should not continue.

References

1. Philip Noel-Baker, *Disarmament* (London, 1926); *The Geneva Protocol for the Pacific Settlement of International Disputes* (London: King, 1925); and *The Present Juridical Status of the British Dominions in International Law* (London: Green, 1929).
2. *Annual Digest of Public International Law Cases* (London: London School of Economics, 1919) continued as *Annual Digest and Reports of Public International Law Cases*.
3. C.A.W. Manning, *The Nature of International Society* (London: G. Bell and Sons, 1962).
4. C.K. Webster, Arnold J. Toynbee et al., *Peaceful Change: An International Problem*, ed. C.A.W. Manning (London: Macmillan, 1937).
5. Frank P. Chambers, *The War Behind the War, 1914-1918* (London: Faber and Faber, 1939) and *This Age of Conflict: A Contemporary World History, 1914-1943* (New York: Harcourt, 1945).
6. Geoffrey L. Goodwin, *Britain and the United Nations* (New York: Manhattan Publishing Co., 1957).
7. Martin Wight, *Power Politics* (London: Leicester University Press, 1946) and Arnold J. Toynbee and Frank T. Ashton-Gwatkin, eds., *Survey of International Affairs 1939-1946: The World in March 1939* (London: Oxford University Press, 1952).
8. F.S. Northedge, *British Foreign Policy: The Process of Readjustment, 1945-1961* (London: Allen and Unwin, 1962) and *The Troubled Giant: Britain Among the Great Powers* (London: G. Bell and Sons, 1966).
9. F.S. Northedge and Michael Donelan, *International Disputes: The Political Aspects* (London: David Davies Memorial Institute, 1971) and F.S. Northedge and

M.J. Grieve, *A Hundred Years of International Relations* (London: Duckworth, 1971).
10. Geoffrey Stern, *Fifty Years of Communism* (London: Ampersand, 1967).
11. Coral Bell, *Negotiation From Strength: A Study in the Politics of Power* (London: Chatto and Windus,1962).
12. James Mayall, *Africa: The Cold War and After* (London: Elek Books, 1971).
13. Alan James, *The Politics of Peacekeeping* (London: Chatto and Windus, 1969).
14. Hedley Bull, *The Control of the Arms Race: Disarmament and Arms Control in the Missile Age* (London: Weidenfeld and Nicholson, 1961).
15. Northedge and Donelan, *International Disputes.*

A Brief History Continued 1972-2002

Brian Porter

The late Professor Northedge took the story of International Relations (IR) at LSE down to 1971. I have continued it to the present on the same scale, although a more detailed history of the Chair and Department since 1924 is in preparation. But fully to understand developments in the 1970s, it is necessary to go back a little.

In 1962 Professor Charles Manning retired after over thirty-two years in the Chair, years in which he had not only created the post-war Department but left his own imprint on its character, reputation and teaching. This is not the place to assess the impact of Manning on the shaping of the discipline and on the many who came under his influence, although those interested should consult Hidemi Suganami's perceptive and judicious enquiry, 'C.A.W. Manning and the Study of International Relations', a welcome and much-needed exercise in rehabilitation.[1]

Manning's successor, Geoffrey Goodwin, was a man of very different stamp. A regular army officer whose career had been cut short by a crippling attack of poliomyelitis, he had read IR for the B.Sc. (Econ.) when the Department was in wartime exile in Cambridge. After three years with the Foreign Office, he had joined the staff at Manning's invitation in 1948. When the Chair fell vacant in 1962, Martin Wight, long seen by Manning as his natural successor, was no longer available, having left the previous year to be Professor of Modern History and Dean of European Studies at the new University of Sussex. In consequence the two leading candidates were Goodwin and Northedge, both internal, and former students of Manning's. Fred Northedge, in some ways, was the better qualified. He had begun his academic career earlier (before the Second World War he had won a scholarship to Oxford to read Classics) and had a greater body of published work to his credit. Goodwin, however, had certain qualities likely to impress the selectors. Although he himself would have been the last to claim outstanding ability as a scholar, or fluency as a writer, he yet possessed natural authority, a mind to get his own way, great conscientiousness as a tutor and supervisor, and a clear idea of how the Department should be run and the direction it should take. In addition, having been educated at Marlborough and Sandhurst, with service in the army and the Foreign Office, he had a rapport with the Establishment, and an understanding of its ways, that Northedge, an industrious and prolific radical of very different social background, neither had nor aspired to.

Hitherto the IR Department had not carried much weight in the internal politics of the School. Manning, with all his subtle brilliance—indeed because of it—had the type of mind and personality that not everyone could readily relate to. He was, moreover, about to embark on that most quixotic last phase of his career, campaigning for the cause of Apartheid on *moral* as well as other grounds to student audiences throughout the English-speaking world, and in the near-revolutionary 'swinging sixties'. Nothing so illustrates his deeply-felt patriotism for his native land (now seen as eccentricity), his courage, and his unworldliness. Goodwin's 'liberal' stance on such matters—around 1960 he gave up speaking to his chief on the subject of South Africa[2]—was virtually a *sine qua non* for exercising influence within the School.

One may cite, as an example of Goodwin's influence, his success in setting up in 1967 the Centre for International Studies (CIS). This he did as Vice-Chairman of the Academic Board (the Chairman being the Director), by securing from the Ford Foundation a 'seed corn' grant of £5,000 to cover the first five years. The idea was to broaden the base of IR by involving representatives of other departments. Applications for Fellowships were invited from distinguished foreign scholars who would be paid a stipend to pursue their research. The results were to be published by Cambridge University Press as a series of LSE monographs. After 1972, although the School would continue to cover overheads, visiting Fellows would be expected to fund themselves.

Money generally was much tighter in the 1970s than in the 1960s. The period of the Robbins expansion had come to an end. Whereas thirteen staff members had been appointed in the 1960s, the figure was down to three in the 1970s, although these three—Michael Yahuda (1973), Christopher Hill (1974) and Susan Strange (1978)—were to render distinguished service to the Department, all three as Convenors and the last two as Montague Burton Professors.

The Montague Burton Chair, although remaining a position of high honour, was no longer in itself the seat of control it had been in Manning's time. Under the School's constitutional reforms of 1962, departments were at last recognised *de jure* (they had long existed *de facto*) with their heads designated 'Convenors'. This represented a shift in the character of higher education which reflected changes occurring in society as a whole. Under the *ancien régime* the Professor was like an absolute monarch. In his thirty-two years in the Chair, Manning had never once called a departmental meeting—there was no need, for he handled everything himself. Students attended classes or seminars strictly by permission of the professor, and Sir Charles Webster, holder of the Stevenson Chair of International History, was in the habit of inviting favoured students to seminars in his own home. The system was, in fact, openly *élitist*. Manning held special seminars for hand-picked students, those he deemed would carry on a sort of academic 'apostolic succession', and so did other teachers for those they felt held special promise. It was an attempt to fit into a modern university structure the age-old transmission of a 'mystery' from the Master to the Apprentice. But now, in the 1960s, a more egalitarian spirit was abroad, demanding not so much a Master as a functionary. Goodwin doubled up as Professor and Convenor until 1969 when Fred Northedge, who that year was awarded a personal Chair, took over the convenorship. From then on each Convenor served for a three-year term. Administratively he or she was the key person in the Department, summoned a Departmental meeting usually twice a term, always sat on the School Selection Committee, was the link between the Department and the School, and made sure that the former was prepared for external auditing. Concentrating these duties in a single person and, for staff of professorial rank, taking them on in turn (although assisted by several sub-committees and working groups) undoubtedly made for a more efficient system when demands on the Department became more pressing and complex. But all through the 1970s (a time of financial crisis in the country as a whole) lack of resources was to frustrate any hopes of expansion. And expansion was essential if Goodwin's intention was to be fulfilled of leaving behind the introspective, role-questioning preoccupations of the Manning years (symptoms of a new discipline's insecurity) and reach out to the world of affairs.

The fashionable, 'up-and-coming' subject of the 1960s was strategy. But not the perennial, 'Clausewitzian'

strategy that Brian Tunstall had taught, but the new and
disturbing concerns of deterrence, the nuclear balance,
pre-emptive strikes, and whether there could be any
rational analysis of power deployed in such
unprecedented forms. Hedley Bull, the brilliant young
Australian philosopher who was eventually to occupy the
Montague Burton Chair of IR at Oxford, had first made
his mark in this field with his seminal study, *The Control
of the Arms Race* (1961), but he had left in 1967 to head
International Relations in Canberra. His place was taken
by a young strategist who was significantly to transform
the prospects of the Department.

Philip Windsor, a product of Merton College, and then
St. Antony's, Oxford, moved to the Institute for Strategic
Studies to work under its Director, Alastair Buchan.
Strongly recommended by Buchan, he joined the
Department in 1965. Equipped with an outstanding
mind, he was not only a lecturer who could hold an
audience spell-bound while speaking without notes, but a
man of high culture who exemplified that unquantifiable
side of higher education—the imparting of wisdom and
learning to the next generation through one-to-one
contact—that the politicians and bureaucrats now trying
to dominate it have never understood nor ever will
understand. Geoffrey Goodwin saw him as his natural
complement, relied much on his judgement, got him
appointed Reader, and hoped he would eventually
succeed to the Chair. It was Windsor's reputation in the
strategic field—he was a valued counsellor to the 'top
brass' of the Ministry of Defence and the
Pentagon—which did much to boost the one-year M.Sc.
(Econ.) programme. Graduates began to come from all
over the world, but particularly the United States, to
study strategy under his direction. This burgeoning of the
graduate intake, with the income it brought, gave the
Department greater influence in the School, and
ultimately led to the expansion that for a decade had been
held back.

Insofar as the Department 'marked time' in the Goodwin years, it was in the field of IR theory. Amongst the senior staff, there was no-one of the calibre of Manning, Wight and Bull to carry this forward. Goodwin himself, although fascinated by Wight's 'International Theory' lectures,[3] which he had attended in the 1950s and freely drew upon, was not sufficiently well-equipped in the history of thought to do anything comparable himself, and Northedge was primarily interested in recent history and institutions. Michael Donelan, noting this absence of soundly-based reflection on core issues, resolved to do something about it and invited IR teachers from other universities, and especially those philosophically inclined, to come to LSE for discussions. And so was born, in 1974, the International Political Theory group which eventually produced three books: *Reason of States* (1978), *Community of States* (1982) and *Condition of States* (1991), edited respectively by Donelan, his colleague James Mayall, and Cornelia Navari of Birmingham.[4] As these titles show, the thinking was state-centred, a tradition which went back to Manning and his preoccupation with 'as if' persons (i.e., states) constituting an 'as if' society, a society 'in idea', subtly controlled by law, convention and morality, which was his main contribution to an understanding of international relations. The wonder was not that there was so much disorder, as that there was so much order in the world. Acknowledging their debt to Manning, his former colleagues conspired to present him with a *Festschrift* entitled *The Bases of International Order*, and after a long gestation this was at last, in 1973, presented to him by Alan James, its editor, in the Shaw Library, and in the presence of many friends, former colleagues and students.[5] Although then in his eightieth year, Manning was as critically combative as ever. Michael Banks, who contributed the final essay to the *Festschrift*, imprudently chose as his subject Manning's own thinking on 'order', and got rapped over the knuckles for getting something wrong. The complaint came in the new, extended Preface he wrote for *The Nature of International Society* when it was reissued in 1975. Fred Northedge, equally imprudently, when reviewing the reissued work for *Millennium: Journal of International Studies*, ventured to make two very mild criticisms about something quite minor. Manning at once sent off a letter to the journal, the crucial wording of which ran: 'I suppose I should be grateful to Professor Northedge, for whereas he had the advantage of an education in International Relations, I did not . . .'.[6] He was always avid to have his work discussed, yet to do so was to risk touching high voltage.

The reissue was Manning's last published work. He continued to lecture to a small group of select graduates (including Hidemi Suganami) until ill-health supervened. Stricken with cancer of the throat, he returned to his beloved Cape Province to die, although mindful of his life's work, he left a sum of money to fund, on a local scale, inter-disciplinary discussions to further an understanding of the subject. He was remarkable not only for acuity of mind, but for physical and moral courage, and for the tenacity with which he defended against critics and enemies (and there were not a few in the School) a subject he had made peculiarly his own. Within a few months of Manning's death in March 1978, Geoffrey Goodwin retired. As the years passed, the incapacitated former major became increasingly irascible. When something upset him, the expression would cloud, the moustache twitch, and the two stout sticks be thrown with a clatter to the floor. But who can tell the frustration and pain of having to throw each leg outwards in order simply to walk? He, too, soldiered on with exemplary courage, and I should like to pay tribute to two very different men, but both inherently kind and generous, to whom the writer, like scores of others, owes an immense debt.

The one-time hope that Philip Windsor would take over had been given up. His intellectual interests and commitment to the tutorial method were too important to him to exchange for the administrative chores and responsibilities of a Chair. Perhaps Geoffrey Goodwin's verdict on him—'brilliant but casual'—was apt. He almost certainly did more good both to himself and to the subject by devoting his remarkable mind to teaching, tutoring and writing.

The Chair was advertised and at a late stage was applied for by someone very different from any who had held it before. Susan Strange was a tough-minded journalist who had graduated in Economics at the School in 1943. Serving first on *The Economist* and then—as Martin Wight had done—on *The Observer* as its UN correspondent, she did not enter the academic profession until 1949 when she went to University College, London, to teach IR under Dr. Georg Schwarzenberger, Reader in International Law. (It testifies to her toughness that whereas some staff suffered a nervous collapse under that academic Captain Bligh, she did not.) From 1965 she spent eleven years with the research staff of Chatham House, working mainly on international finance, and becoming increasingly conscious of the failure of IR and International Economics to engage with each other. Keen to see the economics side of the teaching strengthened, Geoffrey Goodwin favoured her candidature, as did Ralf Dahrendorf, Director of the School and a former European Commissioner, who thought the Department should become more integrated with the world of institutions and policies.

And so she was appointed to the Montague Burton Chair in 1978. She was well aware of the heritage she was entering, and had scant respect for it. Not only did she have something like contempt for Manning's ingenious word-play and subtle philosophising, but was not much impressed with the subject as it had hitherto been taught in the Department. Academics, she held, should come down from their ivory tower and get their hands dirty. Her great ambition was to develop the study of political economy, and not simply at the undergraduate level where it was already taught by Michael Donelan and James Mayall, but through postgraduate teaching, backed up by large-scale grant-aided research programmes. What the world was really about, she argued, was the interaction of state-based political and military power with the largely independent global movements of capital, commerce and information. Holding these views, she was bound to be in vigorous disagreement with the traditionalists over the Department's *raison d'être*. Nevertheless, this energetic, iconoclastic woman had an enormous reputation in the USA and elsewhere, and her influence on the recruitment of graduates helped to fuel the 1980s expansion.

As a result of this growth the decade saw the appointment of eleven new staff (compared with only three in the 1970s) as well as, following the retirement of Professor Northedge in 1984, the creation of a new Chair, advertised the following year. It went to Fred Halliday, an Irishman from Dundalk, who was educated at Oxford and the School of Oriental and African Studies, had a background in scholarly journalism, and was familiar with the Middle East (Arabic being one of his five languages). He had joined the Department as a Lecturer only two years before, and although there were some objections to his precipitate promotion and Left-wing credentials (he had served for fourteen years on the Editorial Board of the Marxist *New Left Review*), his productivity as a writer, versatility as a scholar, and adeptness as a communicator, soon won the admiration of his colleagues. In 1987 he succeeded Professor Strange in her second stint as Convenor. She, however, resigned the Montague Burton Chair in 1988 to join the European Institute in Florence. Although she remained dismissive of its intellectual heritage—and continued to say so with her characteristic candour—she had, through her graduate teaching and such books as *Casino Capitalism*

(1986) and *States and Markets* (1988), fixed the Department even more firmly on the world's academic map.[7]

The next choice for the Chair was a natural one, and more in line with its traditions. John Vincent was impressive. The present writer once heard him regale for an hour a staff/student seminar with a brilliant and fluent disquisition on the subject of 'Race' and all without a note. He had made his mark in the IR world by tackling ethical questions, and notably that which, at the time of writing, is a burning issue: can there be a moral justification for military intervention in the affairs of another state? But it was as much his ebullient personality—Lawrence Freedman recalled his 'broad grin sandwiched between black curly hair and a scarf'[8] and general air of wit and humour—as his powers of analysis which made an impact. Having been only three years at Nuffield, he was reluctant to leave Oxford, but was persuaded it was his duty to come to LSE. He was appointed to the Montague Burton Chair in 1989, and in only the following July became Convenor. Four months later he was dead. Like his mentor, Hedley Bull, he was on to the big things, the true heart of the subject, when he was cut short, and his passing in November 1990 left the study of IR, no less than the Department, deprived of great promise.

John Vincent is the subject of the concluding chapter of a book published by Tim Dunne in 1998 called *Inventing International Society: A History of the English School.*[9] The background to this is curious. In 1981 Professor Roy Jones of the University of Wales wrote an article entitled 'The English School of International Relations: A Case for Closure',[10] and in so doing achieved immortality both for himself and for the 'School' he sought to consign to oblivion. Until then no-one had heard of the 'English School', least of all the 'School' itself. But now, thanks to Professor Jones, everybody is talking about it, and it is being debated and appraised wherever, throughout the world, IR is taught. Was the Department the original home of the 'English School' and Professor Manning its founding father? Or was it Cambridge and the British Committee on the Theory of International Politics? Or was it E.H. Carr? These are questions which cannot be addressed here but should be borne in mind by anyone investigating the Department's contribution to thought.

And so we come to the last ten years and to the current academic scene. Through the 1990s there was unprecedented growth, with twenty new staff appointed. The range of specialisms covered divides into three broad groups. First is the international political core of the subject, represented, amongst others, by Christopher Hill, an Oxford-trained historian and John Vincent's successor in the Montague Burton Chair; Chris Brown, an alumnus who holds a newly-established Chair and has made a reputation in IR theory; and Peter Wilson who has focussed chiefly on the history of international thought and the discipline's academic origins. Secondly the regions of the world are well-covered, as with Europe (five staff, including Professors Paul Taylor and Lord Wallace), the former Soviet Union (Professor Margot Light, the current Convenor), China (Professor Michael Yahuda, the last Convenor), the Middle East (Fred Halliday), and parts of Africa (an area in which, until he departed in 1998 to head International Relations in Cambridge, Professor James Mayall was prominent). And lastly comes a variety of other specialisms, the most comprehensively treated being the international political economy (seven staff), a lasting legacy of Susan Strange. Some of the above participate in more than one group. Space alone curtails a full listing of what is taught and by whom.

Outside the Department, but each directed by one of its staff, are two research units: the European Institute, founded in 1991 and currently run by Paul Taylor; and the Asia Research Centre, directed by Christopher Hughes and set up in 1997 by the late Michael Leifer, a Professor in the Department and specialist in South-East

Asia, and for four years (1991-95) Pro-Director—an ornament to scholarship and to the School. His C.M.G., presented at his hospital bedside a few days before his death, and by the Lord Lieutenant in full uniform, was an acknowledgement that as advisor to the Foreign Office he had done the state some service.

Not to refer to the Research Assessment Exercise (RAE) and the Quality Assurance Agency (QAA) in any account of a contemporary university department would be like writing the history of the seventeenth century without mentioning the visitations of the Plague, but space again forbids.

IR at LSE has come far since the appointment of a sole professor in 1924 and of four lecturers to assist him in 1927 (the date deemed the foundation year of the Department *per se*). Since the 1950s the numbers of students annually enrolled, particularly at the postgraduate level, have probably increased at least four-fold, with a much greater range of what can be studied.[11] By a decision of the School and University, the old B.Sc. (Econ.) was terminated in 1996-97, and a new B.Sc. (IR) introduced. This seemed to demonstrate that IR had come of age, that it was no longer a 'Cinderella' discipline, but one taught and studied by a large Department with a high reputation throughout the world. As though symbolic of this, a move was made (negotiated by Christopher Hill in 1996) to transfer the whole Department from its rather unsatisfactory quarters at the rear of the Old Building, where all the windows faced north-east, to Clement House, fronting the Strand and acknowledged to be the best accommodation in the School.

Yet a returning student from the 1950s would find some things familiar: the Grimshaw Club and its annual dinner (even if sprays of 'love-in-a-mist', which grew like a weed in the Mannings' garden, are no longer placed beside each plate) and the occasional weekend discussion parties at Cumberland Lodge in Windsor Great Park. For these Professor Manning used to think up a theme and get the group in successive meetings to 'ring the changes' on it. (Once it was Nelson's Trafalgar signal with first 'England', then 'expects' and so on down to 'duty', all looked at from every conceivable angle: literal, symbolical, metaphorical, hortatory).

For our returning alumnus, too, the portraits and pictures displayed on the walls of Clement House would summon up remembrance of things past. A splendid oil of Manning conveys well that bird-like quickness and eyes alert with humour. And then there is Fred Northedge in the resplendent robes of a D.Sc. (Econ.), rarest of degrees—the eminent assessor, so the story goes, bleakly contemplating the piled up 'Works of Northedge', plaintively asked, 'Do I *have* to read all this?'. The later professors are all commemorated through framed drawings, although some of these, like Campbell's *Lives of the Lord Chancellors*, could be said to add another terror to death. And then, before reaching Hilary Parker's office—Hilary who, like a Permanent Under-Secretary, has, through a dozen convenorships, cheerfully and efficiently given continuity to the whole enterprise—our visitor would pass that remarkable picture of the Delegates swearing the Oath of Ratification to the Treaty of Munster (or Westphalia). Perhaps, to counter the danger that IR will eventually be transmogrified into Global Sociology, it would be no bad thing if each Convenor, on entering office, swore an oath before this picture to uphold the study of what it represented.

And the new building itself, not just its furnishings, has much to commend it. The rooms, spacious, airy, and south-facing, and overlooking Aldwych and the Strand, provide vistas and views which themselves evoke thoughts on IR. To the far right is Bush House, from where Fred Northedge and Geoffrey Stern would regularly tell the world about the world.[12] Before us, in the centre, the magisterial figure of Mr Gladstone, a statesman who believed in Europe as a Christian Commonwealth and in the duty of the Great Powers to uphold the moral order, looks out on a world clearly not much to his taste. Finally, well to the left, before the once-blitzed church of St. Clement Danes, stand statues of the two greatest proponents of the defensive and the offensive in aerial warfare: Lord Dowding and Sir Arthur ('Bomber') Harris. Even the majestic neo-classical pile of Australia House may point a moral or adorn a tale.

The writer recalls walking past it, on his way to the School, on 26 January 1988. It was the bicentenary of the first British settlement in Australia and he was expecting an 'open day' with welcoming portals flung wide. Instead they were barred, and the building ringed by police. Confronting the police was a motley crowd, in varied garb and with threatening mien. A group of them bore placards proclaiming: LESBIANS FOR A BLACK AUSTRALIA. One wonders what Professor Manning would have made of that. One likes to think that out of it he would have got a Cumberland Lodge weekend.

References

1. See Hidemi Suganami, 'C.A.W. Manning and the Study of International Relations', *Review of International Studies* 27, no. 1 (2001): 91-107.
2. Geoffrey Goodwin to the writer, probably June 1960.
3. These famous lectures were eventually edited and published as Martin Wight, *International Theory: The Three Traditions*, eds. Gabriele Wight and Brian Porter (London: Leicester University Press, 1991).
4. Michael Donelan, ed., *Reason of States: A Study in International Political Theory* (London: Allen and Unwin, 1978); James Mayall, ed., *Community of States* (London: Allen and Unwin, 1982); and Cornelia Navari, ed., *Condition of States* (Milton Keynes: Open University Press, 1991).
5. Alan James, ed., *The Bases of International Order: Essays in Honour of C.A.W. Manning* (London: Oxford University Press, 1973).
6. The letter was shown by Professor Manning to the writer, but did not appear in *Millennium: Journal of International Studies* having been suppressed by Geoffrey Stern. This led to more caustic correspondence!
7. Susan Strange, *Casino Capitalism* (Oxford: Blackwell, 1986) and *States and Markets* (London: Pinter, 1988).
8. Obituary, *The Independent*, 7 November 1990.
9. Tim Dunne, *Inventing International Society: A History of the English School* (London: Macmillan, 1998).
10. See Roy Jones, 'The English School of International Relations: A Case for Closure', *Review of International Studies* 7, no. 1 (1981): 1-13.
11. In the early 1950s, of the total B.Sc. (Econ.) list, around twenty students specialising in IR graduated *per annum*. At present graduations in the B.Sc. (IR) run to 45-50 *per annum*. At the M.Sc. level some 90 qualify each year in IR, and some 60 in the Politics of the

World Economy. In addition, some 130 research
students are registered for the Ph.D. or M.Phil.
12. From Bush House Fred Northedge and Geoffrey Stern
regularly broadcast on current events for the BBC
World Service. Most of these commentaries went out
at about 6 a.m. and were commended to everyone by
Professor Manning, an assiduous listener.

Martin Wight and the Abolition of War

Roger Morgan

This previously unpublished short text by Martin Wight (1913-1972) is characteristic of his style of argument: clear, forthright, and reinforced by apt quotations and examples from history. It is also typical of much of Wight's work in another way: as he himself admitted, he was too much of a perfectionist to find it easy to complete long manuscripts.[1] Two of his major books, the expanded second edition of his seminal 1946 study *Power Politics* and the collected essays of his later years, were only edited and published posthumously,[2] and the work widely regarded as his *magnum opus*, *International Theory*, based on his famous LSE lecture-course, was only reassembled and published in 1991.[3] It was therefore on his shorter writings, lectures and broadcasts that Wight's high scholarly reputation rested during his lifetime. In his time as a Reader at the LSE International Relations Department (1949-61), he was undoubtedly one of its outstanding 'stars'.

The short paper presented here was written in 1959 for a specific and limited purpose: it was Wight's comment on a proposition developed by the American scholar Walter Millis that war should be abolished.[4] Responding briefly, as he did, Wight was obviously not in a position to deploy the whole range of his thinking about war. He could have discussed the issue of 'just' and 'unjust' wars, or extended his reflections on what would today be called 'wars of national liberation', contrasting them with 'wars of humanitarian intervention': he certainly had strong views on these issues, as well as on preventive wars or 'wars of fear', but they were not central to the question of war's abolition. However, the main points of his argument here—that wars can serve a constructive function in international society, that the causes of war are often misrepresented, that any desirable political change comes at a price, and that war is inevitable unless international anarchy is replaced by 'some form of government'—are fully in keeping with his general views on the subject of war.

His views, that is, in the period of his mature scholarship, after the Second World War. As is well known, during the war Wight was a Christian pacifist, and a conscientious objector to military service and to killing:[5] his later insistence on the omnipresence and even the positive value of war in international society could perhaps be seen as denoting, in a sense, the zeal of the convert. In his LSE lectures, for instance, Wight introduced his discussion of 'Theory of War' quite categorically:

> War is the central feature of international relations, though in academic study this is often forgotten. If this is too Realist a statement, we can say instead that war is the ultimate feature of international relations, as revolution is the ultimate feature of domestic politics.[6]

In *Power Politics* he went even further, describing war between nations as one of the 'institutions' of international society: 'the institution for the final decision of differences'.[7]

In arguing that war was not only inevitable but often constructive—though he took it for granted that it was 'morally detestable, politically wasteful and inefficient as a means of regulating international life'[8]—Wight was consciously contradicting one of the fundamental tenets of the academic discipline of International Relations (IR). In 1910 the pioneering Carnegie Endowment for International Peace declared that its first objective was 'to hasten the abolition of international war', and optimistically added that as soon as this end was achieved, its resources would be diverted to other necessary reforms. The first academic posts in IR, including the Wilson Chair at Aberystwyth (1919) and the Cassel Chair at the School (1924), were endowed to promote the aims of the League of Nations, including the ending of war.[9] Even the British Foreign Office, during the brief period in the mid-1960s when Hedley Bull was head of its Arms Control and Disarmament Research Unit, commissioned a study of how a completely disarmed world would look, and whether the abolition of armaments would mean the abolition of war.

The research proposal developed by Walter Millis thus represented a strand of mainstream thinking in IR, but Martin Wight responded to it from an individual position which he had worked out, and defended, with originality and tenacity. Like many of his other readers and hearers, the American author of the original 'Memorandum on the Abolition of War' must have been stirred into further reflection by Wight's response. He may have thought, for instance: why does Wight argue at one point that wars sometimes create their own dynamics and get destructively and pointlessly out of hand (like the Thirty Years' War in its last decade), whereas there are other wars—both world wars, in Wight's reasoning—which must be fought to a finish? Again, what exactly is Wight saying in his third argument against the abolition of war, when he maintains that every political benefit has its price, and that history 'appears to offer difficult choices'? Certainly some choices in world politics are very hard indeed, but surely not all of them are like that, and in some cases the cost/benefit ratio may even be perfectly straightforward? Moreover, does Wight actually believe

in the possibility of some sort of world government, as he
hints in his concluding paragraphs, or is he really saying
that, since this is utopian, war will continue in certain
circumstances to be not only inevitable but also
constructive?

This polemical little note (written, we should repeat,
for a particular purpose) illustrates another aspect of
Wight's intellectual make-up: his fascination with
European traditions of thought, exemplified in his
throwaway reference to Erasmus. As Timothy Dunne has
argued, it was this fascination which took Wight away
from his Readership at the LSE to become the first Dean
of the School of European Studies at the new University
of Sussex.[10] It is highly significant that Wight chose to
combine the Deanship with a Chair of European History
rather than of International Relations, though he did
design an undergraduate syllabus in IR which could have
been a model both for new and for old universities.[11]

One measure of Martin Wight's impact on the
International Relations Department at the LSE is the
dedication with which his former colleagues and pupils
have laboured to ensure the preservation of his ideas in
print. Although the time he spent in the department was
relatively short, his influence on the development of the
subject must be ranked among the very highest.

References

1. See Wight's letter in Timothy Dunne, *Inventing International Society: A History of the English School* (London: Macmillan, 1998), 48-49.
2. Martin Wight, *Power Politics*, 2d ed., eds. Hedley Bull and Carsten Holbraad (Harmondsworth: Penguin for the Royal Institute of International Affairs, 1979) and *Systems of States*, ed. Hedley Bull (London: Leicester University Press, 1977).
3. Martin Wight, *International Theory: The Three Traditions*, eds. Gabriele Wight and Brian Porter (London: Leicester University Press, 1991).
4. Walter Millis (1899-1968) was, at the time he sent his 'Memorandum' for Wight's comments, a Fellow at the Center for the Study of Democratic Institutions, the reformist Californian think-tank. He was a prolific author on strategic and international questions: the LSE library catalogue lists 19 works by him, including 'The Abolition of War' (1963).
5. Dunne, *Inventing International Society*, 51-52, 65-66.
6 Wight, *International Theory*, 206.
7. Wight, *Power Politics*, 112.
8. Wight's, *On the Abolition of War: Observations on a Memorandum by Walter Millis*, p. 54 in this volume.
9. Roger Morgan, ed., *The Study of International Affairs: Essays in Honour of Kenneth Younger* (London: Oxford University Press for the Royal Institute of International Affairs, 1972), 273.
10. Dunne, *Inventing International Society*, 66.
11. Roger Morgan, 'A European "Society of States"—but Only States of Mind?' (the twenty-fifth Martin Wight Memorial Lecture), *International Affairs* 76, no. 3 (2000): 560-61.

On the Abolition of War: Observations on a Memorandum by Walter Millis[*]

Martin Wight

My central criticism of this paper is that 'the war system' never comes clearly into focus. If we are to discuss abolishing war from international society, it is necessary to agree about the function war has fulfilled in international society, because it will probably be necessary to provide that this function be performed by some other means. 'The war system' is described in this paper wholly in negative, apocalyptically negative terms. It is illustrated, almost exclusively, by the Axis Powers' use of war for aggressive nationalistic interest [in the 1930s]. But it takes two sides to make a war. Resistance to the Axis Powers was as much part of the war system as

---

[*] This is an edited reproduction of a hitherto unpublished paper entitled 'Observations on Mr Millis's Memorandum on the Abolition of War' written by Martin Wight in 1959. The memorandum's author, Walter Millis, had asked Wight for comments on his working paper, which proposed a study of the subject. Millis later published a book on the subject, Walter Millis and James Real, *The Abolition of War* (New York: Macmillan, 1963). We would like to thank Gabriele Wight for her generous permission to publish this text.

aggression by the Axis Powers. It was, in theory, open to the American government and people to take a practical step towards 'abolishing the war system' by capitulating to Japan immediately after Pearl Harbour. But the American government and people chose instead to perpetuate the war system by offering resistance. It appears to be the consensus of mankind [. . .] that the United States deserved well of the human race by so choosing.

I have four main criticisms of your memorandum. Firstly it ignores the positive or constructive functions of war in international society, which might be summarised thus:

(i) To effect desirable change. Cavour's aggressive war against Austria in 1859, and Garibaldi's conquest of Sicily and Naples, have been generally approved by posterity. Some who have no love of imperialism would include the Mexican War, or the British Conquest of the Sudan, in this class. And there is one kind of desirable change that has been so important in international history that it deserves separate mention:

(ii) To establish independence. I think it would be true to say that, from the Revolt of the Netherlands down to 1900, not a single newcomer to international society has been able to gain admission without asserting its right by war, like the United States, or creeping in as a result of somebody else's war, like Rumania in 1856 or the new states of Eastern Europe in 1918. The limiting instance would be Belgian independence, achieved after a suppressed war between the Dutch and Belgians and joint intervention by the Powers to coerce the Dutch. Since 1900 there have been the examples of independence peacefully attained by Norway, Iceland and the Philippines, but the great majority of newly enfranchised states owe their independence more or less directly to the two World Wars. Tunis and Morocco profited from France's defeat in the Indo-China war, as Guinea profited from France's inability to suppress the Algerian Revolt.

Perhaps Ghana alone offers an example of peaceful attainment of independence among the Afro-Asians.
(iii) To preserve independence. Is it to be denied that the battle of Bannockburn, and the career of Joan of Arc, and the resistance of the Montenegrins to Ottoman conquest, and of the Spaniards against Napoleon, and the resistance of the Greeks to Mussolini's invasion, and of the Finns to Stalin in the Winter War, show one side of the war system? Given a multiplicity of sovereign states lacking a political superior, their readiness to go to war is the ultimate guarantee of their continued independence. In this sense, the war system has been the implicit guarantee of Swiss or Swedish neutrality since 1815. That is to say, the general recognition that either of these countries would fight like blazes against any direct violation of its neutrality has made even a Hitler reckon that the costs of conquering them would outweigh the advantages. [. . .] The preserving of independence could be regarded as an illustration of the war system's positive function in blocking *undesirable* change. Another illustration of this function would be:
(iv) To preserve the balance of power. All this means, in its old and proper sense, is joint action by the majority of states to preserve their common freedom ('the liberties of Europe', etc.) against an attempt to establish a universal monarchy. The succession of grand alliances, from Queen Elizabeth plus Henry IV plus the Dutch down to Roosevelt plus Churchill plus Stalin, show the war system functioning to maintain the life of international society, against the succession of threats to transform it into an ecumenical despotism.
I assume that it is not necessary to meet the sophistry of the argument that, since every war has two sides, there can be no agreement on what is 'desirable' or 'undesirable' in international politics. This was the silly-clever scepticism that undermined the Versailles Settlement by asserting that there is no such thing as justice and that all you ever have is the relationship of

victors and vanquished, top-dogs and bottom-dogs. I assume that there is broad agreement among intelligent men that it was not a pity that Spain did not succeed in crushing the Dutch rebels, that it was not desirable that Turkey should continue to misgovern the Balkan peoples in the 19th century, and that it was a good thing that Louis XIV did not win the War of the Spanish Succession, and that Hitler did not win the Second World War.

If it were the core of your argument that the state-system regulated by the balance of power has *now* become obsolete because of nuclear weapons, like John H. Herz in his latest book,[1] I should not join issue with you, or at least the argument would be on different ground. But your unqualified condemnation of the war system is retrospective, and this is why I have wanted to assert its positive and constructive function. Of course war is morally detestable, politically wasteful and inefficient as a means of regulating international life. There is nothing new in recognising this. Erasmus was saying so in 1515.[2] There is no sense in which war became 'obsolete' in 1916 in which it had not always been 'obsolete', i.e., provoking humane and sensitive men to ask what the hell was the good of it. Most great wars seem to have reached a middle point where the original issues have become blurred or forgotten and the struggle carries on by a malignant momentum of its own. The Thirty Years War did after the Peace of Prague in 1635, the Spanish Succession War did after Britain extended her war aims in 1707. Yet it is very questionable whether the peace offers of the winter of 1916-7 marked such a point in the First World War. None of the original issues of the War had then been decided. Germany was not prepared to retrocede Alsace-Lorraine; not even the German Chancellor von Bethmann Hollweg was ready to relinquish control over Belgium. I can only record disagreement with the statement that 'even the victors were to gain nothing for their peoples or their regimes comparable to what they paid for the last two terrible years of the war'. [. . .] Would Poles, Czechs, Yugoslavs, Transylvanian Rumanians, Lithuanians, Latvians, Estonians, Finns agree with it? It was precisely in the last two years of the War that the military empires of Eastern Europe fell to pieces and the subjugated peoples found their national freedom. What did Britain get out of the War? The German colonies, control of the Middle East, the sinking of the German fleet. Only the first of these was in their grasp by 1916. It was in the last two years that the Ottoman Empire was destroyed and the Arabs were liberated. A negotiated peace in 1916 would have left the German navy intact, an abiding menace to the British—and the Americans.

This brings me to my second main criticism. Not only does the part played by power in international politics seem to me to be underrated in this paper, but the intractability of international conflicts as well. Let me give three examples.

(i) 'Once the great military organisations and armaments are removed, there would be nothing left for them to fight about'. The biggest international blood-letting since 1945, apart from the Korean War, was the massacres that attended the partition of the British Raj into India and Pakistan. Fear of its reoccurrence is, of course, a principal explanation for India's Kashmir policy. Neither of these emergent states had great military organisations or armaments. Could it be seriously contended that Israel and Egypt would have nothing left to fight about, i.e., that their mutual hatred would be eliminated, by their being disarmed? Indeed, it seems possible that total disarmament might make an energetic and socially advanced state like Israel seem *more* rather than less dangerous in the eyes of its backward neighbours, since the resources released from armaments would go into building up its economic and industrial strength. In other words, it is not armaments that cause war, but human passions and conflicting interests.

(ii) The illustration of Latin America seems to me to
leave out the essential point: Latin America has a
policeman and nurse-maid in the shape of the United
States. (Not always effective, either: the efforts of the
U.S.A. and the League of Nations, sometimes combined
and sometimes conflicting, to stop the Chaco War [1932-
35], are instructive.) There are other examples in
international history of a kind of sub-system, or pocket,
with a localised international society and a localised
balance of power. The Arab world today; Italy under the
Spanish and Austrian ascendancies. Moreover, the Latin
American countries are at a low level of political
integration and economic development, and this makes
their pressure upon one another's frontiers less than the
average of international society as a whole.

(iii) I don't know any British student of international
affairs or recent history who agrees with your criticism of
Article X of the Covenant, or with the explanation of how
the Allies failed after 1919.[3] It was not the Allies' 'whole
system of military dominance' that was at fault, but the
inadequacy of the system, or to be more precise, the lack
of intelligence with which it was maintained and applied.
This is why Churchill called the Second World War 'the
unnecessary war'. To say that 'their exclusive
preoccupation with military force *incited* the totalitarian
challenge' seems to me the reverse of the truth. Stimson,
Simon, Chamberlain go down in history as having been
too little concerned with military force. The Japanese
went ahead in Manchuria, and the Germans in Europe,
only after having sounded out the chances of military
resistance and assured themselves that none was
forthcoming. But this is a well-worn debate, and there is
no need to rehearse it at length.

My third main criticism concerns a more general point
of principle. It is a common fallacy in political discussion
to suppose that desirable results can be obtained without
paying the price. It is a kind of neglect of the laws of
historical causation, taking two complementary forms.

Either one is so aghast at the price exacted that one neglects to observe that the goods have after all been delivered. Or one is so keen on the goods to be delivered that one overlooks that a price is to be paid.

'Could any sane man, standing in 1945 amid the vast ruins of Berlin or Hamburg, of Tokyo or Hiroshima, conclude that the deliberate organisation of major war was any longer a rational or even possible means of conducting the relations of states?' I submit that a sane man would have humbly reflected, first of all, that this destruction was the result of 'the deliberate organisation of major war' by the United States and Britain. And he would have reflected upon the purpose of it. And he would have humbly concluded, I think, that this was the price to be paid that the chimneys of Auschwitz should smoke no more and the Japanese should not be in occupation of California. History, it seems to me, is not a fun–fair offering give-away prizes and free drinks to men of goodwill. It appears to offer difficult choices. At that time it offered peace, at the price of letting Hitler and Tojo rearrange the world, or the curbing of Axis barbarism, at the price of the Second World War.

Fourthly, a theoretical study of how international society might be expected to work given the hypothesis of general disarmament would be interesting and valuable. But I venture to suggest that it would be interesting and valuable in proportion as it does not assume that disarmament will solve most of the world's other problems as well. What your paper calls 'the war system' has dominated international society only because there was no better institution to dominate it.

In other words, I am with those who believe that stable order is a priority needed in international affairs to effect peaceful change, and therefore I see the function war has performed in preventing undesirable change as more essential than its function in bringing desirable change. The provision for and balance between these two

functions seems to me the core of any theoretical attempt
to abolish war.

The alternative to war in some form is government in
some form; anarchy has at no time and in no place been
resolved without the establishment of a monopoly of
power. It is fairly safe to predict that this would be the
result of a Third World War, provided a sufficient degree
of social organisation survived. The predominant
remaining Power will almost certainly establish a
monopoly of atomic weapons, as William H. McNeill
argued in his *Past and Future* several years ago.[4]

The past year has brought a dim hope that this might
come about, without war, by concert between America
and Russia to prevent the growing threat to their joint
atomic monopoly. It seems to me chimerical to suppose
that 'disarmament' can mean anything except reduction
plus concentration of certain kinds of armament in the
hands of an 'international' authority. If such an authority
were simply an American-Russian dyarchy in disguise
(and it is very difficult to see what else it could possibly
be), it would be necessary to temper one's theoretical
approval of it by sober consideration of (a) the intrinsic
instability of dyarchy, which raises the classical problems
of divided sovereignty, and (b) its disagreeableness from
the point of view of those who are subjected to it against
their will, of whom in the present instance France and
China afford obvious examples.

Your picture of a world from which war has been
abolished by agreement seems on the whole pastorally
anarchic and self-regulating, and I cannot believe in it.
But the need for government, i.e., controlled central
power, obtrudes itself when you say that 'new forms of
international consultation and control' might be
necessary, and when the likelihood is envisaged that
certain troublesome small states might need to be coerced
by 'the combined pressure of the great states'.

I should like to see the need for international
government moved into the centre of the picture. Once

there, everything else falls into place around it; without it, everything else continues to drift uncoordinated. The *general* theoretical problem is: 'What is the minimum change in international politics to set up an effective "international" authority capable of preventing private war and according protection to states? And what exactly is the word "international" going to mean in this context?' The *particular form* in which this question presents itself at the present moment is this: 'What is the minimum change to secure that the control of atomic and nuclear weapons is monopolised by a single "world" authority? And what is the least unpleasant and burdensome form that this single "world" authority can be expected to take?'.[5]

References

1. John H. Herz, *International Politics in the Atomic Age* (New York: Columbia University Press, 1959).
2. Desiderius Erasmus, 'Dulce Bellum Inexpertis' (1515). A translation can be found in *The 'Adages' of Erasmus: A Study with Translations*, ed. Margaret Mann Phillips (Cambridge: Cambridge University Press, 1964).
3. The controversial Article X of the League of Nations Covenant reads 'The Members of the League undertake to respect and preserve . . . the territorial integrity and existing political independence of all Members. . . .' Millis was clearly arguing that this explicit commitment to the totality of the territorial settlement agreed at the Paris Peace Conference of 1919, and the obstinacy of the victorious Allies in enforcing it by 'military dominance', were direct causes of the aggression by the totalitarian powers in the1930s.
4. William H. McNeill, *Past and Future* (Chicago: Chicago University Press 1954).
5. After the last sentence Martin Wight added this concluding thought: 'In other words extrapolate the Baruch Plan into contemporary conditions, and adapt accordingly'. The Baruch Plan was a US initiative proposed in mid-1946 to outlaw nuclear weapons and to internationalise global stocks of fissile material for use in peaceful nuclear programmes.

Hedley Bull and the Case for a Post-Classical Approach

James Der Derian

'An institution is the lengthened shadow of one man'.[1]

No single event defines a life, but from my first to my last encounter with Hedley Bull, the compass of my academic life was set. Even when our paths diverged, Bull's antipodal nature—the Oxford robes barely cloaked an Australian nonconformism—would continue to influence my future choices.

The first encounter took place in his Balliol College study. Barely into the first term of a political philosophy graduate degree at Oxford, I had already managed to burn my way through two tutors; one was interested only in John Rawls, the other in dry sherry. The word in the dining hall was that the Montague Burton Professor was revamping the International Relations (IR) programme for the better, that not only was he a good tutor and lecturer, but unlike most Oxford dons he actually knew how to run a graduate seminar. I requested a meeting. After a few pleasantries, Bull got down to it: what IR courses had I taken as an undergraduate in North America? To this day I believe that my acceptance into the IR program hinged on my response. After pausing to consider how I might inflate the actual truth of the matter, I hesitantly answered: 'only one'. After a couple of wheezy puffs, he asked me why. I confessed to boredom and a chronic inability to distinguish a dependent from an independent variable. One chortle later, Bull took me on as a student, sealing the decision with an invitation to the drink's party that he hosted each year for new graduate students in IR.

At the drink's party, I got my first glimpse of the idiosyncratic side of Bull. The IR program had not yet been colonised by North American students, and all twenty of us along with the odd, some quite odd, assortment of dons could fit into the Master's Garden. A new student acquired Bull's ear, and confidently expounded on the general neglect of Leon Trotsky's writings in the field of IR. Bull listened, rocking from heel to toe. I learned later to decipher this pendular motion as a kind of physical wind-up to an imminent verbal salvo. However, the fan of Trotsky took Bull's bemused silence as an opportunity to dig himself a deeper hole, into which he stacked concepts for the rescue of bourgeois IR, like the 'law of uneven and combined development', 'permanent revolution', and 'dual power'. Just as the widening arc of Bull's rocking threatened to plant a Liverpool kiss on Trotsky's young acolyte, Bull spoke: 'Hmmm, yes, yes, and when I was an undergraduate, we thought the divine light shone forth from Stalin's arse'.

My last encounter came as a letter, a mixed signal that would have a powerful and lasting impact. Dated 17 January 1985, the letter was a response to an earlier request that he read a new draft introduction of my Oxford dissertation that I was then revising for publication. He wrote:

> Do finish your revised thesis and publish it before you become bored with it. I am very suspicious of your 'post-classical approach to International Relations theory'. It seems rather pretentious and likely to get you into

> trouble. Does your thesis really need this? I have always felt that it would be better standing on its own as an orthodox account of the evolution of diplomacy than as an exercise in some mysterious new methodology which will have to be shot down in due course by some sceptical critic as all the previous methodologies have been. If you would like me to read it, however, I should be delighted.

He then informed me of the bad news: 'To cut a long story short, I have had a malign tumour lodged in my spine'. At the bottom of the typewritten letter, he penned in his barely readable script a final message, one that I interpreted not as an afterthought but as a supplement, the excess of writing that undoes the coherency of the given text. He wrote: 'Stick to your guns, and do what <u>you</u> think is important, not what others want you to do'.

Bull died three months later. He never read the introduction but it didn't matter; weighing his advice, I jettisoned the 'post-classical approach'. A small portion of it did, however, see the light of day as part of an introduction to the 1988 special issue of *Millennium: Journal of International Studies* on *Philosophical Traditions in International Relations*.[2] When the *Millennium* editors came calling again for a Special Edition on the Department's anniversary, I tried to consider the options as Bull might have. The editors specifically asked for my 'impressions, recollections and thoughts on his mentorship, and the way it did or did not influence your take on the field of IR'. From my encounters with Bull it should be obvious that he had little use for sycophants of any stripe. However, the editors' *coda* to the request gave me an opening: 'the more unconventional and innovative the piece, the better'. I detected an echo of Bull's take-it-and-leave-it advice to me; indeed, it was not unlike waving a red flag in front of a bull. I decided there could be no better way to honour Bull as well as the editors' needs than to make my case for a post-classical approach.[3]

My strategy is simple: I first present a synopsis of the classical approach as the 'lengthened shadow of an individual'; that is, as I learned it from Hedley Bull in four years of tutorials, lectures, seminars, and dissertational supervision, and as I subsequently compared that knowledge to future surveys of the 'English School'. Second, I introduce what I consider to be the shortcomings of the classical approach, which entail a post-classical supplement of *identity, representation*, and *epistemes*. Third, I consider three historical and philosophical questions that distinguish the post-classical from the classical approach. How does the formation and interaction of identity and difference, among self and groups, define international relations? Second, how do written, visual, and other forms of representation act as both constructive and destructive forces in international relations? Third, what new post-classical thinkers might guide us from the present to the past and back again, and provide us in the interpretive process some wisdom about future dangers and opportunities?

The Classical Approach to International Relations

Hedley Bull brought to the classical approach an appreciation of theory. Whereas Martin Wight, Herbert Butterfield and others thought historical reasoning and empirical techniques were sufficient for their diplomatic investigations, Bull plunged headfirst in the theoretical debates of the day. His definition of IR theory was deceptively simple: 'the leading ideas that have governed and do govern our thinking about International Relations'.[4] And the three goals of IR theory were plainly laid out: 'to expound what those ideas are, to relate them to their historical context, and to examine their truth and their bearing on our present political concerns, in relation to past practice and to present practice'.[5] But it was in the theoretical historicisation—and hence differentiation from the behaviouralists—that the depth of the classical approach emerges. Bull clearly thought the philosophical-historical investigations of the classical approach superior to methodological-behavioural proofs because they were time-tested, self-reflecting, and judgemental.

The classical character of his version of IR theory can be traced back to the origins of theory itself. People once travelled to Delphi, one of the most sacred sites in ancient Greece, to pursue knowledge of the truth, an act that came to be described by the joining of the Greek terms *theoria* and *horao* for journey and an attentive contemplation.[6] We should not make too much of linguistic origins, but it would appear from time immemorial that theory required a journey, to seek out a distant truth, to look outside oneself, to reach for (if never entirely achieve) a balance between one's own world and the world beyond. From my first tutorials with Bull, I have come to identify theory with travelling, often to very strange places, in pursuit of highly elusive truths, and with the greatest insights coming from the journey itself rather than the final destination.

Second, Bull took culture seriously. Culture is as old as the first attempt to cultivate a seed, a germ, or an idea. Matthew Arnold placed the concept on a pedestal, writing in 1866 in his influential *Culture and Anarchy*, that culture is 'a pursuit of our total perfection by means of getting to know . . . the best which has been thought and said in the world'.[7] In a realm so imperfect as IR, it is not surprising that culture long suffered from neglect. It has, however, enjoyed a resurgence of attention in both the theoretical and policy sides of IR.[8] Bull construed culture as the glue as well as the proof of his key concept, the international society.[9] Contrary to the realist view that states are engaged in a perpetual struggle for power in an international anarchy, the classical approach upholds a belief in an international society composed of states tied together by a common set of values, rules, and institutions. According to this view, an underlying 'international system' or 'states system' provides a level of interaction such that one state's actions will impinge upon another's. But something more than the contiguity of physical action is at work in an international society: a common culture. The formation of an international society has been dependent upon the expansion—sometimes peaceful, more often not—of predominately Western cultural values, codes, and symbols.

Bull identifies three primary cultures at work in the international society.[10] He distinguishes the elite 'international political culture'—the formative and reflective attitude of international society—and 'diplomatic culture'—the ideas and beliefs held in common by official representatives of states—from a more universal, cosmopolitan 'world culture', which is identified by modernity. World culture is still a 'culture of the dominant Western powers' but one that is moving to absorb non-Western elements and values. In turn, all three of these cultures could be sub-divided into 'a common intellectual culture—such as a common language, a common philosophical or epistemological outlook, a common literary or artistic tradition—the presence of which served to facilitate communication between the member states of the society'; and 'common values—such as a common religion or a common code—the presence of which served to reinforce the sense of common interests that united the states in question by a sense of common obligation'.

Third, before the study of norms became the norm of IR theory, Bull was doing ethics, in both the most general sense of investigating the principles and rules of conduct which guide international relations, but also as an a priori critical attitude that must attend all theoretical inquiry. Ethics has suffered from neglect in IR, but the subject has recently reappeared in the liberal/constructivist analysis of norms as an influential set of principles, rules or values, as well as in the critical/post-structuralist study of ethics as part of a normative process by which theory helps to construct the world through acts of perception, narration, and inscription.[11] Bull was speaking both languages before they had become theorised into opposing camps. He advocated objectivity but openly declared it unattainable. Bull thought it a laudable but unlikely prospect that we might be able to separate how we see, tell stories, and write about the world, from how we judge what is right or wrong, possible or not in that world. Ethics is as much the product of *how* as it is the object of *what* we study in IR. Moreover, ethics tightens the bond between theory and practice, making us partially, if not individually, responsible for what we make of the world. Bull's radical view on this in the preface to *Anarchical Society* bears repeating: 'inquiry has its own morality, and is necessarily subversive of political institutions and movements of all kinds, good as well as bad'.[12]

Bull's classical triangulation of theory, culture, and ethics work as a kind of Global Positioning System for his wide-ranging historical and empirical investigations of international relations. They help the reader position themselves in the text, in the complexities of history, and in the rapidly changing present. More broadly, they also help us to understand how our own positions, as scholars and students, writers and readers, are influenced and fixed by how we study the world. Bull was very aware of the pull of power on knowledge, and of how the key questions in IR of objectivity (the where, what, and when) are inflected by subjectivity (the who, why, and how). Bull contributed a philosophical self-consciousness to the classical approach, but he stopped at the edge of the Enlightenment map. If we are to find and begin to understand the sea monsters that lurk beyond the edge, however, more is needed: a post-classical approach that understands how the representational powers of the maps themselves help to determine who is friend or foe, when and how wars will be fought or ended, and whether or not just the West but the rest of the world constitutes the international society.

Identity

A post-classical approach reopens the question of identity. A dictionary definition might emphasise the distinguishing characteristics of an individual, or the essential sameness of a group. Everyday events can give us a good sense of the importance of identity. Some identities we choose, while many seem to choose us: one needs state identity to vote, photo identity to get on a plane, national identity to go from one country to another, and for some unfortunates, proof-of-age identity to buy an alcoholic beverage. Identities come with benefits and costs: differences in gender and racial identities show up in disparate income levels, rates of incarceration, even probabilities of execution. The focus on identity shifts in different fields of knowledge: a psychologist might focus on the attitudes and the perceptions of the individual; a sociologist on the formation and behaviour of group identity; an anthropologist on the rituals and ceremonies of a tribal or communal group; a linguist on the common sign-system of a language group; and a political theorist on the legitimacy of a governmental identity. Long before constructivists in IR caught on to the question of identity, British philosopher David Hume wrote of its pertinence in 1739: 'Of all relations the most universal is that of identity, being common to every being whose existence has any duration'.[13] In other words, identity is fundamental to all.

The identity question in international relations raises the ante. The most general function is the relationship between those we identify as us and those we identify as them, as self and as other, as identity and as difference. Identity is a constitutive part of international relations, unifying as well as dividing whole peoples. The effects of identity can range from familiarity and friendliness, to indifference and tolerance, to estrangement and hostility. Understanding or not understanding others' identities can result in appreciation or denigration, accommodation or separation, assimilation or extermination. Together, the formations, functions, and effects of identity can draw physical boundaries between peoples, as well as metaphysical boundaries between life and the most radical other of life, death. They can separate humans from God. And they can build the fence that makes good neighbours, as well as the wall that confines a whole people.

The ultimate reason to study the concept of identity in international relations is that 'we' make war and make peace with 'others'. These others might be newly encountered people from across an ocean or over a mountain range. They might be all-too-familiar people, who once were fellow humans, reliable allies, friendly neighbours, or even likeable kin. They might be a projection of some aspect of ourselves. But for one reason or many—or, as we seem forced to relearn in every generation, for no reason at all—they come to be recognised as the 'other': barbarian, infidel, heretic, savage, revolutionary, traitor, racist, sexist, lunatic, alien, cyborg. In turn, the collective identity of 'us'—the citizen, the patriot, the believer—becomes dependent upon these differences. These historic encounters of identity and difference have created fundamental physical, metaphysical, and representational boundaries in and of international relations.

Representation

Identities do not form in a vacuum. Social, political and historical factors are important influences. But in every case there is at work a formative relationship between identity and representation. Representation generally refers to an action or a symbol that stands for or expresses something else. In traditional textbooks on politics, representation usually refers to the process in which an elected or appointed person expresses the interests of a greater number of persons. We need to expand that notion to include the study of symbolic and metaphorical representations, which like identity itself are formed out of a relationship to something different. We need to examine how representation and identity are mutually constitutive, in the sense that both are defined by an interaction of differences: we become who we are by how we represent ourselves as different from others. This is the second arena in which a post-classical approach is required.

This becomes clearer when we get more deeply into the similarities and differences between political and linguistic uses of representation. Just as representatives in a democracy 'stand for' others who are not present in a parliament or legislature, words, images, symbols, signs, and other representations stand for the complex realities of the world. There are similar difficulties with the realities of war and peace: they cannot all 'fit' into a single representation. Ambiguities and uncertainties can arise from acts of perception and interpretation. To paraphrase a past President of the United States, one person's freedom fighter is another person's terrorist. But how do we know what distinguishes one from the other? How, for that matter, do we know that freedom fighters, unlike fire fighters, fight *for* rather than *against* freedom?

Whether representations say what they mean and mean what they say is a key question (a question that might also be raised about some political 'representatives'). Some philosophers of language claim that reality is transparently reproduced by representations: representations reflect reality. When I write 'mouse', these philosophers would say that I have clearly indicated a furry rodent with four legs and a tail. Others believe that reality can be distorted or obscured by the context, intentions, and method of representation: representations refract reality. When I write mouse, such a philosopher would say that I could have meant a rodent, a timid person, or, perhaps because I mis-clicked with a different kind of mouse, a louse. And the most radical interpreters of language go so far as to say that reality is entirely created by representations: representations construct reality. When I write mouse, they see a relationship of signs which produce an image of a rodent rather than, say, that of a house, because of internally governed linguistic conventions which generate meaning without any reference to an external material reality.

Representations can do all three things: reflect, refract, and construct reality. As well, a powerful synergy between representations and identity is often in operation. They both are produced and sustained by difference. To put it simply, representations and identities are informed and constructed by a relationship to something different. Understanding the nature of this mutually constitutive relationship is fundamental to understanding international relations. This is especially true in the context of war and peace, where the representation and constitution of identity are all too often accompanied by a rigidifying violence that often defies purely rational explanations.

War, as an organised form of violence, is age-old. So too are efforts to end, prevent, and outlaw war. Yet, as Geoffrey Blainey remarks in the opening lines of *The Cause of War*, 'For every thousand pages published on the causes of wars there is less than one page directly on the causes of peace'.[14] After discussing a host of other explanations, Blainey speculates that war is simply more interesting, more newsworthy than peace. War is simply more difficult to ignore than peace. Probably even Hedley Bull would have agreed with Leon Trotsky, when he stated that 'You may not be interested in war, but war is interested in you'. We could go further, and say that war is not only more newsworthy and interesting than peace: it is more representative of the long history of violence and conflict in international relations. The story

James Der Derian

of war must be told, but with an awareness that in the constant telling and retelling of war we also delimit and ignore the possibilities of peace.

No politics, especially international politics, stands above or outside of representation. The role of representation is a matter of philosophical controversy, from the early dialogues in ancient Greece between Socrates and the Sophists to more modern debates between different schools in IR theory. But there would probably be wide agreement that the number and pace of critical representations in international politics are rapidly outstripping human comprehension: microprocessor speeds double every year, ubiquitous surveillance intrudes into our public and private lives, 500 channels are available on television sets that now outnumber toilets in American households.

We can see how the introduction of identity and representations raises concerns and questions to which the classical approach has not and probably cannot respond. What roles have national, religious, cultural, social, racial, gendered, political and other identities played in the preparation, execution, and termination of war? How, in turn, have new forms of representation, from mass newspapers to radio speeches to popular films to video and the Internet, created new identities? Who controls representations and identities? Are they freely chosen, or chosen for us? Is peace possible without some deeper understanding of how we produce, in the very act of understanding of who 'we' are and what we are not, the conditions for war or peace, of fear, hate, and resentment, or accommodation, mediation, and reconciliation? Can there ever be a truly secure identity? Can there ever be a peace that is not merely a temporary absence of war? At what cost? These are the type of questions that the classical traditions of IR can hardly understand, let alone answer.

The Classical Traditions

History involves a dialogue of the living with the dead, or rather the 'undead', those representatives of the past who haunt the present with invocations of tradition. Tradition can be a collection of doctrines, a type of behaviour, or even a way of regarding others. From its Latin origins in Roman law, *tradere* (meaning to 'hand over' or 'pass on', to its invocation by the powers that be, tradition has been the means by which the continuity, the authority, and—one hopes—the wisdom of the past is transmitted or handed down to the present.

In IR, the classical approach bears the cross of tradition more so than any other IR theory. From Martin Wight on, it has located three powerful traditions in international relations: the Realist, Rationalist, and Revolutionist traditions. Following the names of their respective seminal thinkers, Niccolò Machiavelli (although Bull preferred the more 'modern' Thomas Hobbes), Hugo Grotius, and Immanuel Kant , they are also identified as 'Machiavellian' (Realist), 'Grotian' (Rationalist), and 'Kantian' (Revolutionist).[15] Although rooted in particular moments in history, these traditions acquire a 'classical' status because they transcend the constraints of time and place to provide transhistorical insights about the theory and practice of international relations. They continue to shape not only how scholars think about the world, but also how leaders and diplomats practice international politics according to the principles embodied by the traditions. Before challenging the traditions, it is important to understand, if even in shorthand, their analytical value.

The Machiavellians (or Realists) were described by Martin Wight as the 'blood and iron men'.[16] In their ranks were thinkers like Thomas Hobbes and Georg Friedrich Hegel, and leaders like Frederick the Great and Otto von Bismarck, whose ideas and lives became the source for 20th century realist theorists like E.H. Carr and Hans

Morgenthau. Their view of human nature was starkly
pessimistic; consequently, human relations were full of
'sin, suffering, and conflict'. In *Leviathan*, Hobbes
famously extrapolated from human nature the causes of
conflict: competition, diffidence, and glory that give rise
to wars of gain, safety, and reputation. This meant that
international politics, without a 'common power to keep
all in awe', was indistinguishable from a state of nature
or anarchy: men are in a 'condition called war', *bellum
omnium contra omnes*—'every man against every man'.[17]
International society was, at best, a convenient fiction to
cloak the naked pursuit of power in legal niceties and
diplomatic formality. Justice was whatever was in the
interests of the strongest party. Foreign policy consisted
of cunning and coercion. The endless struggle for power
assured a history marked by repetition and recurrence.
The 'other' had no rights, except to be conquered if weak.
In short, might makes right.

The Grotians (or Rationalists) are the 'law and order
men'. Some of the more influential Grotian thinkers were
John Locke and Edmund Burke; famous leaders were
Franklin Roosevelt and Winston Churchill. They took a
more moderate view of human nature than the
Machiavellians, and saw good as well as bad, in a state of
constant tension. Unlike Hobbes, Locke discerned
evidence of comity and goodwill in a state of nature.
Property rights and contract law were expanding from
the domestic to the international realm. Human and
international relations, improved through reason (by
great men) and paternal vigilance (by great powers),
could produce some sense of historical progress. Most
importantly, the innate nature of humans for sociability
provided the germ for an international society, to be
nurtured and protected by institutions like a balance of
power, diplomacy and international law which might
mitigate the excesses of sovereign states pursuing
national interests. Conflict among states would still arise,
but in the Rationalist perspective social and economic

intercourse elevated the value of cooperation. Without a world government, wars break out, but they were 'just wars', fought according to shared principles of legitimate authority and proportionality. Foreign policy was best served by honesty and trust in negotiation. The 'other' had some rights under tenuous universals like natural law, but not the right to obstruct trade or to limit the expansion of 'civilisation', for these are the forces bringing peace to international society. In short, reciprocity rules.

The Kantians (or Revolutionists) are the 'subversion and liberation men'. Their view of human nature as redeemable by education and acculturation was optimistic, and the source of a conviction that the anarchy of independent states was an obstacle for the progressive movement towards a community of mankind. Composed of thinkers who wrote of the world as it ought to be, the pantheon of Kantians was small but influential, and came with a wide range of views on how to change an unjust system of states. At one end there were evolutionists like Woodrow Wilson who advocated constitutionalist reforms for the states system, and at the other revolutionists like Vladimir Lenin who called for its eradication. The Kantian perceived a Manichaean international politics, of a world divided between good and evil, the saved and the damned, the oppressed and the oppressors. The ends of foreign policy was to end the state itself, so as to replace national interests with the interests of humanity. Therefore, propaganda and subversion were preferable to negotiation and compromise for the goal of human perfectibility. The only just war was holy war, leading to total victory. The right of the 'other' was to assimilate—or risk extermination. In short, right makes might.

Classical international theorists are well aware that there are risks as well as benefits to a theoretical approach based on traditions. In both the original formulation by Martin Wight and in the reassessment by Hedley Bull, caveats accompany the traditions of international theory.[18] They are both aware that traditions work because they reduce the complexities of the past in order to transmit it in a comprehensible form to the next generation of thinkers. The traditions are not to be construed as some magic key to open the door of history, or a pigeon-hole into which contemporary events and figures should be stuffed. Wight and Bull view them as general paradigms inspired and embodied by seminal thinkers who provided a useful set of historical *descriptions* (of what happened), political *prescriptions* (of what ought to be), and, in some instances, theoretical *inscriptions* (of what can be thought and written). As Hedley Bull noted in his lectures, not even Machiavelli was a Machiavellian. These representative thinkers were much deeper, more reflective observers of their respective times than any synoptic tradition can possibly convey. Their status as 'classical' thinkers reflects an ability to transcend their own time, to offer some timeless wisdom for world politics. But it also reflects a certain openness, even ambiguity to their thought, that allows for transhistorical interpretation. This is why these traditions remain useful analytical and interpretive tools for understanding present as well as past practices and principles of IR.

Nonetheless, there remain theoretical hazards. The traditions can be abused to distort the past into expedient justifications of the present. They can make the present a mirror image of the past. This would impoverish international relations theory by a 'presentism', where the past neatly adds up, like a mathematical formula, to the present. Moreover, with the accretions of time and power, traditions can also fossilise into 'natural histories' that weigh heavily on the living, and provide fewer as well as thinner insights as contemporary IR goes through radical transformations. At such moments, counter-traditions take on an appealing form.

The Post-classical Epistemes

As well as providing a new set of historical guides, a post-classical approach adopts stricter philosophical guidelines for defining the classical traditions. It takes the traditions seriously, perhaps even more so than the classical international theorists, because the traditions are treated as constitutive rather than merely reflective forces in international politics. According to this approach, the traditions do not simply record and transmit the history of world politics: they are part of a constant making and unmaking of history through interrogation, interpretation, and narration. The traditions act as narratives, or stories of the past that limit as well as enable a set of interpretations for the present. Traditions are used to interrogate rather than confirm current conventions and assumptions in IR, by setting up dialogues with alternative, counter-traditional perspectives. It is a first step towards the kind of critical, historical reasoning that makes the reader an ethical producer rather than a neutral consumer of knowledge.

Traditions and counter-traditions in the post-classical approach serve as historical markers for the emergence of particular discourses, or authoritative statements that shape international politics, which are then further reduced to pithy aphorisms, like 'prepare for war if you desire peace', or 'might is right'. Discourses, narratives, and traditions determine what can be said, who can say it, and when it can be said with power and persuasion, legitimacy and authority. When they are elevated into dominant paradigms that explain events to the exclusion of all other explanations—one story is naturalised into the truth—we can, and shall in this case, call them *epistemes* (from the Greek term for 'knowledge'). Drawn from the work of Michel Foucault, the French philosopher of systems of thought, *epistemes* are defined as the foundational discourses that establish the origins, methods, and limits of systems of understanding.[19] For a traditional or counter-traditional discourse to take on an epistemic power, it must be debated by powerful figures, spread by new technologies of communication, routinised by custom and habit, institutionalised by formal practices, and finally (but not necessarily sequentially), philosophically and consciously rendered by criticism, sometimes even outright opposition, into a (counter-)tradition.[20]

The enduring concepts and institutions of international relations, from power and sovereignty to international law and diplomacy, took shape during the time Machiavelli, Grotius, and Kant were writing. But innovations in transportation (railroad and steamship), communication (telegraph and radio), and production (assembly line and machines) ushered in an industrial age that forever altered how humans make war and peace. Moreover, the realities of world politics are increasingly generated, mediated, and even simulated by new means of representation, further distancing them from some original historical moment or original meaning. Moving at speed from the industrial to the informational to the virtual age, the classical traditions are hard-pressed to keep up. How can we expect Machiavelli, Grotius or Kant to further our understanding of permanent states of neither war nor peace (cold war), new technological forms of warfare (information war, cyber-war, net-war), para-wars that rely as much on the metaphor as the reality of war (trade war, drug war), and the whole array of wars that do not fit into the traditional categories and explanations (race war, class war, gender war, culture wars)? New forms and multiple sources of conflict often seem to resist comprehension through the traditional paradigms, not least because they all place a premium on the value of reason and the secular to explain international politics. The failure to anticipate the end of the cold war—as well as the lack of a vision after it—is the most recent and notable testimony to this resistance. Alternative security regimes, feminisms, the accelerated flows of information, capital, refugees, critical social movements, trans-national crime, environmentalism, media politics, and fundamentalism are just some of the more powerful challenges which have suffered from theoretical neglect by traditional approaches.

To enhance the critical pluralism needed to comprehend newly multipolar and multicultural times, I offer a new *troika* of post-classical counter-traditions: the Nietzschean (Friedrich Nietzsche); the Gandhian (Mahatma Gandhi); and the Beauvoirian (Simone de Beauvoir).[21] In keeping with Wight's penchant for alliteration, they will also be called the Relativists, Revelationists, and Irenists.

The Nietzscheans, or Relativists, are the 'will to power men'.[22] Like the Realists, they view the world as a site of permanent contestation of the will, the most vital of life forces: 'life is a consequence of war, society itself a means to war'.[23] But the will to power cannot be reduced, as the Realist would, to self-preservation: 'Life itself is will to power; self-preservation is only one of the indirect and most frequent results'.[24] Therefore, the will to power should not be confused with a Machiavellian lust for power. When repressed, the will to power can produce a reactive and resentful longing for only power, leading to the triumph of nihilism.

But under conditions of freedom, will to power is an active and affirmative force which revalues all imposed values. It pits individuals against themselves, not others, in an act of self-overcoming. Neither human nature nor the state of nature can be defined as a given, or a timeless fixity; only something that has no history can be defined. Nor can they be seen as existing as some kind of prior condition or permanent cause of strife. They are powerful effects of the 'death of God',[25] like the end of first principles and the rise of modernity, all of which have led to the construction of new systems of faith based on rationality as well as systems of politics based on

sovereignty. Nietzsche attacks these and all other
demonstrations of a 'will to a system'. Life is a contest of
wills and a desire for recognition. Systems might promise
protection but they also corrupt life, leading to the
decadence of mass society and mastery over others,
rather than a self-becoming and mastery over oneself.
Adolf Hitler is the arch-example of the former; Vaclav
Havel, the latter. The will to power is repressed,
domesticated, and bureaucratised by the dominant
system of modernity, the nation-state, producing all
kinds of pathologies: 'madness is rare among individuals;
in entire nations it is common'.[26] In foreign policy, the
will to power is projected as the desire for security,
producing a collective resentment of others and the
uncertainty they represent. This, in turn, triggers further
insecurities. Real peace only comes when states stop
preparing for war, even if done in the name of self-
defence. Real security only comes when one recognises
and learns to live with a multitude of perspectives and
the insecurity of all values. Like the Realist, the Relativist
views history as discontinuous yet recurrent, an endless
cycle. This does not, however, lead to despair or
amorality. Rather, the 'eternal recurrence' entails an
ethical challenge to accept that one will relive the
consequences of one's actions, either in smallness or
greatness. From God to Rational Man, from Empire to
Republic, from King to the People, the history of IR has
been an effort to resecure the centre, to keep at bay
anarchy, chaos, and difference. Rather than substitute a
new foundational centre, the Nietzscheans offer a
philosophy of relativism and perspectivism, an ethics of
revaluation, and a politics of pluralism to negotiate the
ambiguities and paradoxes of a life in which the only
certainty is death. In sum, right is always relative to
might.

The Gandhians (or Revelationists) are the 'truth and
faith men'. Founding father of India, leading proponent
of non-violence, and ardent believer in the revealed truth,

Gandhi is the name-sake of the Revelationist counter-tradition. He has earned emblematic status to represent what often goes under-represented in the study of war and peace: the profound role of faith, love, and truth in struggles of national liberation and anti-imperialism as well as in the non-violent resolution of conflict and the reconciliation of belligerents. All too often religion is studied in the social sciences as the enemy of reason and a threat to peace. In its most extreme fundamentalist forms this has been and continues to be the case for some religious movements. But there is another story to be told—one that gets lost in the exhibitionism of fundamentalist violence. Testifying to the cross-cultural as well as cross-faith power of the Revelationists, Tolstoy in Russia, Martin Luther King in the US, and the Dalai Lama in Tibet share an alternative vision to the pervasive violence at the core of the international system. The aim of the Revelationists is to end conflict through non-violent, persuasive, empathetic means. The means matter as much as the ends. The Gandhian idea of *satyagraha* (literally, 'truth in firmness') best captures this sense of means as ends-in-the-making. Truth is not to be found in reason, a state, or a culture but in the revelation of the will of God. The Revelationists do not, however, call for holy war. The force of truth cannot be used to inflict pain or punishment upon others because humans are incapable of absolute knowledge of the truth: 'what appears to be truth to the one may appear to be error to the other'.[27] One cannot be sure enough to impose one's views upon. Moreover, truth is tempered by love for the whole of humanity; Gandhi refers to *satyagraha* as the force which is born of truth and love. In the Revelationists' struggles against conditions of injustice and oppression, symbolic power levels the playing field, and gives this counter-tradition a pragmatic power. The symbolic powers of ritual of sacrifice, catharsis through tragedy, and purification through suffering (*tapasya*) are augmented by the reciprocal powers of forgiveness, tolerance, and compassion. Together, these powers of the Revelationists are practically applied through a range of political actions: civil disobedience, non-violent strikes, hunger strikes, occupations, demonstrations, amnesties, and commissions of truth and reconciliation. A world without war—defined as political, economic, and religious violence—is the goal, but this means one must endure rather than inflict pain, be ready to lay down your life rather than to take others. In short, righteousness makes non-violent might.

The Beauvoirians (or Irenists) are the 'gender and peace' women. Simone de Beauvoir's book, *The Second Sex*, was the first to offer a systematic feminist critique which linked the perpetuation of inequality and violence to masculine *cultures* and *representations*, rather than to fixed human natures or biological differences.[28] Two of her most famous epitaphs are: 'One is not born but rather becomes a woman'; and 'Representation of the world, like the world itself, is the work of men; they describe it from their own point of view, which they confuse with absolute truth'.[29] Since Beauvoir, feminist counter-traditions have been fruitful and multiplied, ranging from existentialist to essentialist, standpoint to empirical, psychoanalytic to post-structuralist, liberal to backlash. Each of these feminisms differ on how gender is viewed, as natural, constructed, or just androgynously irrelevant. But most strands of feminism continue to share, more or less, a critique of masculinity which links patriarchy to war; hence the emblematic tag of 'Irenists', from Irene, the Greek goddess of peace. In this counter-tradition, men are not necessarily the 'bad' warriors, and women the 'good' peacemakers, although some essentialist feminists do blame testosterone and credit motherhood to imply such a position. More often, Irenists represent a theoretically sophisticated attempt to understand how certain representations and constructions of gendered identities, both male and female, have perpetuated conditions of injustice and violence. Historically,

patriarchy has enforced such conditions through a
politics of exclusion (public space is for men, private
space for women); theories of psychoanalysis (men are
enabled by the penis, women disabled by envy and
hysteria); discriminatory legal codes (the 'law of the
father' keeping wealth and power in the hands of the
men); and privileging one side of a binary opposition
over another (mind over body, strong over weak, rational
over emotional as natural conditions of gender). The
Irenists expose, so to speak, masculinist values posing as
universalist principles. In IR, the autonomous self, the
sovereign state, the principle of self-help are all
interpreted as masculine values, in contrast to feminine
ones of interdependence, cooperation, and caring. Irenist
foreign policy revalues neglected issues like reproductive
rights and equality for women as well as disarmament
and peace-making. The Irenists subvert the hierarchy of
war when they take a set of gendered identities and
values that appear biologically fixed, and reveal its
historical, cultural, and representational contingency. In
short, care makes might.

Identity through Dialogue

A post-classical approach does not construe epistemes as
frozen artefacts of the past. This approach treats the
present itself as a continuous dialogue, between a past
that is open to interpretation and a future that is open to
construction. Moreover, in this dialogue, where neither
the past nor the future is a given, the question of identity
is always present and pressing. The identity of the
subject—that is, the self, the sovereign state, or
international society—is constituted through this
dialogue. The subject is made 'real' by the meaning that is
conferred upon it by the dialogue between past and
present. This post-classical approach, which recognises
that identity is always under construction, grants a

greater role to history. But it also suggests that there might be a wider range of options for the future than is usually presented in international relations.

The Russian linguist Mikhail Bakhtin used the model of language to raise the importance of dialogue in the formation of identity. He suggested, as Hume did of identity, that a 'dialogism' is at work in all human relations. He challenged the closed Marxist orthodoxy of 'dialectics' with the open concept of the 'dialogic', using language as the model for how we recognise the very necessity of difference for understanding ourselves and others:

> There is no first or last discourse, and dialogical context knows no limits (it disappears into an unlimited past and in our unlimited future). Even past meanings, that is those that have arisen in the dialogue of past centuries, can never be stable (completed once and for all, finished), they will always change (renewing themselves) in the course of the dialogue's subsequent development, and yet to come. At every moment of the dialogue, there are immense and unlimited masses of forgotten meanings, but, in some subsequent moments, as the dialogue moves forward, they will return to memory and live in renewed form (in a new context). Nothing is absolutely dead: every meaning will celebrate its rebirth.[30]

In the act of communicating and negotiating meaning with others, we constitute the self. This entails forward as well as backward perspectives: every responsive act depends upon prior as well as anticipates future discourses.[31] This means that identity is not just some internal, psychological creation: identity requires difference. We are dialogically constructed in discursive communities, whether it is a group of people debating one version of their past over another, historians arguing over the rise of Nazism, or IR theorists engaged in a variety of specialised languages. In other words, we are more dependent upon discourse with others for our own identity than we tend to realise. In Bakhtin's words, 'The psyche enjoys extraterritorial status'.[32] Yet, in world politics, the state continues to 'enjoy' the status of a highly territorial, sovereign identity. Bakhtin would respond that when the monologue of one tradition dominates a dialogue among many traditions, hard, fixed, conflictive identities tend to follow.

These insights on dialogues between the present and past, the self and other, as well as between and among the traditions, might take us one step closer to my earlier call in *Millennium* for a post-classical approach that can help us to understand '*why* a particular tradition develops in a specific historical moment, *how* it makes the world intelligible, the *source* of its persuasive power, and the *cost* of a tradition which outlives its heuristic value'.[33]

We can see how these theoretical questions might have a variety of pragmatic implications. Consider the first (amidst the mess of the second) Gulf War. Was it fought to keep the US strong and our gas tanks full? Was it an effort to counter an illegal intervention by Iraq into Kuwait, which required a re-establishment of a regional balance of power best achieved through a coalition of forces? Was it a struggle of good against evil, Western civilisation and democracy against the barbarism and dictatorship of Saddam Hussein? Or was it fought, as the first President Bush declared, 'to kick the Vietnam syndrome': to renew, in other words, a collective identity of Americans willing to intervene in distant conflicts? Each of these questions represents a tradition, and it is in the dialogue between them, rather than the imposition of any single one, that might yield the best explanation of the Gulf War. Moreover, the philosophical as well as pragmatic aim of a dialogue is to provide what a monologue cannot: an informed plurality of perspectives which might then produce both public and ethical support for the toughest policy decisions faced by national leaders of when to and not to go to war.

Studying war and peace as a dialogue leads inevitably to the question of identity. A dialogical approach means that we do not treat history and meaning as 'other', as something to conquer, transcend or end, but as something with which we continually engage in the process of forming our own identity. The extent to which we make history or history makes us is a critical question for our identity as a citizen of a particular country. Does the identification of one belief with the truth define particular identities? In times of war and terror, do we choose the identity of patriot, or is it chosen for us? Does the very creation of a collective identity require war? Why would it? Just how free are 'we' to make peace?

The Devolution of Hedley Bull

I often find myself wondering, what would Hedley Bull now make of a post-classical approach? Or of IR in general? Difficult to say, but past encounters might again provide some clues. I can still see his eyebrow raised in scepticism when I first outlined in 1980 a master's thesis that appropriated alienation theory for an inquiry into diplomacy. A couple of years later I escalated my original misdemeanour into a major felony, by proposing to use the ideas of the French thinkers Sartre, Barthes, and Foucault for a doctoral dissertation on diplomacy as a system of estrangement. But by then Bull was more than an accomplice to the crime. He anticipated Huntington's clash of civilisations by over a decade, lecturing on historic encounters of identity in his 1981 Trinity Term lectures on 'Ideas of the Unity of Mankind'.[34] As supervisor of my doctoral dissertation, 'On Diplomacy: From States of Alienation to the Alienation of States', he combined muted praise with benign neglect, until it came down to the wire, when he hosted at home evening-long sessions of sentence-by-sentence critiques, softened by the consumption of fine Riesling wines. He picked up the pieces after a parlous viva defence, at which my examiners, Michael Howard and Adam Watson, so rattled my cage that I failed to hear them announce that I had passed, but figured out as much when they invited me to Bull's house for a celebratory garden party (how this invitation was conveyed in advance of the viva, given the strict Oxford guidelines that there be no communication between the examiners and the supervisor, remains a mystery). Based on past experience, I suspect that Bull would have carried on as before, slightly out of step and yet always one step ahead, because he knew the old paths better than just about everyone else, and because he was not about to waste much time trying to break new ones.

References

1. Ralph Waldo Emerson, 'Self-Reliance', in *Essays and English Traits, The Harvard Classics*, vol. 5, ed. Charles W. Eliot (New York: P.F. Collier and Son, 1909-14[1841]), 17.
2. James Der Derian, 'Introducing Philosophical Traditions in International Relations', *Millennium: Journal of International Studies* 17, no. 2 (1988): 189-93. In this essay I marked the arrival of post-structuralist and post-marxist as well as post-classical approaches in IR. I have since made the case for a post-structuralist approach. History has rendered a verdict, an unjust one that will come back to haunt IR (yes, like a spectre), on the viability of a post-marxist approach.
3. I wish to emphasise that this essay outlines an 'approach' rather than attempts to develop a full-blown theory or a school of thought—at a time when Bull is commonly identified as a fully-paid up member of the 'English School' now being touted as a 'globally recognized brand name'; Barry Buzan, 'The English School as a Research Program: An Overview, and A Proposal for Reconvening' (paper presented at the BISA Conference, Manchester, December 1999) [http://www.leeds.ac.uk/polis/englishschool/buzan99.htm] (21 September 2003). It might be useful to remember that Bull dismissed the notion of IR as a disciplinary 'school' and thought, at best, that it represented a subject-matter. Equally, my focus on Bull is delimiting: many thinkers shaped the classical as well as post-classical approaches. However, based on my marching orders from the *Millennium* editors as well as my own view that the English School is a

'pseudo-institution' (as Hedley Bull, following Martin Wight, called the United Nations), i.e., laudable aspirations without commensurate powers, my interpretation adopts the Emersonian view that all institutions are the 'the lengthened shadow of one man'.

4. Wight coined the term 'international theory', which Bull also used but came to prefer 'theory of international relations' as he put it, for reasons of precision since it is the relations that are international rather than the theory. It might still be an ambiguous term, but what Martin Wight says about the language of Grotius equally applies to 'international theory': that a 'fruitful imprecision' better reflects the subject under scrutiny. See Martin Wight, *International Theory: The Three Traditions*, eds. Gabriele Wight and Brian Porter (London: Leicester University Press, 1994), xii and 1; and Hedley Bull, Lecture Notes to Theory and Practice of International Relations 1648-1789, author's files.

5. Ibid.

6. This etymology of theory is drawn from James Der Derian, *On Dipomacy: A Genealogy of Western Estrangement* (Oxford: Blackwell, 1987); Martin Heidegger, *The Question Concerning Technology and Other Essays*, trans. William Lovitt (New York: Harper, 1977); Costas Constantinou, *On the Way to Diplomacy* (Minneapolis, MN: University of Minnesota Press, 1996); and the always insightful suggestions of Michael Degener.

7. Matthew Arnold, *Culture and Anarchy* (Cambridge: Cambridge University Press, 1932), 6.

8. On the theory side, see Friedrich Kratochwil and Yosef Lapid, *The Return of Culture and Identity in IR Theory* (London: Lynne Rienner, 1996); on the policy implications of culture, see Samuel Huntington, 'The

Clash of Civilizations?', *Foreign Affairs* 72, no. 3 (1993): 22-49.

9. See James Der Derian, 'Hedley Bull and the Idea of Diplomatic Culture', in *International Society after the Cold War*, eds. Rick Fawn and Jeremy Larkins (London: Macmillan, 1996).

10. Hedley Bull, *Anarchical Society: A Study of Order in World Politics* (New York: Columbia University Press, 1977), 303-35 and Hedley Bull and Adam Watson, eds., *The Expansion of International Society* (Oxford: Clarendon Press, 1984).

11. For liberal and constructivist approaches, see Peter Katzenstein, ed., *The Culture of National Security: Norms and Identity in World Politics*, (New York: Columbia University Press, 1996); Andrew Moravcsik, 'Explaining International Human Rights Regimes: Liberal Theory and Western Europe', *European Journal of International Relations* 1, no. 3 (1995): 157-89; and Jeffrey Checkel, 'International Norms and Domestic Politics: Bridging the Rationalist-Constructivist Divide', *European Journal of International Relations* 3, no. 4 (1997): 473-95. For examples of critical and post-structural approaches, see David Campbell, *National Deconstruction: Violence, Identity, and Justice in Bosnia* (Minneapolis, MN: Minnesota University Press, 1998) and Neta Crawford, *Argument and Change in World Politics: Ethics, Decolonization, and Humanitarian Intervention* (Cambridge: Cambridge University Press, 2002).

12. Bull, *Anarchical Society*, xviii.

13. David Hume, *A Treatise of Human Nature*, vol. 1, 1874, 323.

14. Geoffrey Blainey, *The Causes of War* (New York: Free Press, 1973), 3.

15. Wight, *International Theory*.

16. These forensic composites are mainly drawn from the lectures and writings of Martin Wight and Hedley Bull, and, as can be discerned from the casual use of 'men' for all actors in IR, they were not much touched by feminist thinking.
17. Thomas Hobbes, *Leviathan*, ed. Richard Tuck (Cambridge: Cambridge University Press, 1991 [1651]), Chapter 13.
18. Hedley Bull, 'Martin Wight and the Theory of International Relations', in Martin Wight, *International Theory*, ix-xxvii; Brian Porter, 'Patterns of Thought and Practice: Martin Wight's "International Theory"', in *Reason of States: A Study in International Political Theory*, ed. Michael Donelan (London: Allen and Unwin, 1978), 64-74; and Michael Donelan, *Elements of International Political Theory* (Oxford: Clarendon Press, 1990).
19. 'By episteme, we mean, in fact, the total set of relations that unite, at a given period, the discursive practices that give rise to epistemological figures, sciences, and possibly formalized systems'; Michel Foucault, *The Archeology of Knowledge and the Discourse on Language*, trans. A. M. Sheridan Smith (New York: Harper & Row, 1976), 191. See also Michel Foucault, *The Order of Things: An Archeology of the Human Sciences* (New York: Vintage, 1973).
20. It might be somewhat romantic but useful nonetheless to note that Machiavelli was banished from public life (after a short spell of torture and imprisonment), and only achieved political notoriety after a barrage of anti-Machiavellian tracts. Grotius wrote some of his best work while in prison for high crimes against the state. And even the relatively timid Kant once suffered censure from the Prussian King Frederick for his writings on religion. It is important

to remember the often insurgent origins of traditions that come to dominate international politics.

21. Just as there are other candidates for the traditions (e.g., Thomas Hobbes, who Bull preferred over Machiavelli, Adam Smith or Karl Marx), so too with the counter-traditions (e.g., Frantz Fanon, Simone Weil, or Hannah Arendt). The choices I have made should be judged by their ability to help us navigate through the issues, complexities and dilemmas of contemporary international politics.
22. Friedrich Nietzsche, Will to Power, #53.
23. Friedrich Nietzsche, Beyond Good and Evil, trans. Walter Kaufmann (New York: Vintage, 1989), 21.
24. Friedrich Nietzsche, Twilight of the Idols, trans. R.J. Hollingdale (Harmondsworth: Penguin Books, 1968), 25.
25. Friedrich Nietzsche, The Wanderer and His Shadow.
26. Walter Kaufmann ed., The Portable Nietzsche (New York: Viking Press, 1954), 71-72.
27. Mohandas Karamchand Gandhi, Teachings of Mahatma Gandhi, ed. Jag Parvesh Chander (Lahore: The Indian Printing Works, 1947), 494.
28. Simone de Beauvoir, The Second Sex (New York: Knopf, 1952).
29. Ibid., 301, 161.
30. Mikhail Bakhtin as quoted in Tzvetan Todorov, Mikhail Bakhtin: The Dialogical Principle (Minneapolis, MN: University of Minnesota Press, 1984), 110.
31. Mikhail Bakhtin, The Dialogic Imagination: Four Essays by M.M. Bakhtin, ed. Michael Holquist (Austin, TX: University of Texas Press, 1981); Todorov, Mikhail Bakhtin; and Paul de Man, 'Dialogue and Dialogism', in The Resistance to Theory (Minneapolis, MN: University of Minnesota Press, 1986), 106-15.
32. Mikhail Bakhtin, Marxism and the Philosophy of Language (New York: Seminar Press, 1973), 39.

33. Der Derian, 'Introducing Philosophical Traditions', 190.
34. On several occasions, the last in a letter of 7 February 1984, Bull suggested that we cooperate in a study of how such encounters shaped IR. Inspired by his 1981 lectures, I have been teaching a course and updating a textbook for the last ten years, 'Representations of War, Peace and Identity', which begins, as Bull did, with the Greeks and Barbarians and ends with the Humans and Cyborgs. An hyperlinked version will soon be available, my final tribute to Bull.

Decency and Tragedy in International Relations Thought: The Legacy of Philip Windsor

Hugh Dyer

Few writers on international relations would think to view their subject in terms of decency and tragedy; fewer among those who take a realistic (not to say Realist) approach to questions of war and strategy; and fewer still consciously do so because it concerns the survival of humanity and the articulation of values. Philip Windsor did.

Of these two themes, decency is one that Windsor rarely employs explicitly, and while he makes specific use of tragedy, there is limited elaboration on the topic itself. However, both thematic motifs are useful in providing a general framework for appreciating his work. In the ordinary meaning of decency one might find the kernel of a widely shared aspiration for relations among human individuals and societies: 'something like a common humanity rooted in cultural diversity'.[1] This does not necessarily imply agreement or empathy but does entail respect or at least tolerance. Neither does it involve cultural relativism, but rather a common humanity engaged in becoming. That decent relations are not easy to achieve, and that there is no convenient recourse to universals—no teleological realisation of the 'species being'—to impose such relations, points us towards an appreciation of the tragic element in human life. Confronting tragedy, rather than evading it, requires recognising the dangers of pride or arrogance, the base instinct of retribution, and the need to make amends on both counts. Tragedy is endemic, and an understanding of it can be, as Windsor says in literally his last word, an act of liberation.[2] His work does not offer us a particular theory or method for this understanding, but rather a kind of lens. Through this lens can be seen features of hope and desperation, which any observer of international relations might recognise, but which few are able to describe as well as Windsor.

This discussion of Philip Windsor's intellectual contribution to the study of international relations, his legacy or heritage, if you will—though he would not have; there was an ego of course, but not of that sort—rests partly on his last book, *Strategic Thinking: An Introduction and Farewell*, which also represents his 'last word', at least on one of his central concerns.[3] One might also look to 'Cultural Dialogue in Human Rights' as a reference point for his later thinking, as well as for an indication of his range;[4] this piece is one of twenty reprinted in a recent collection of his essays, *Studies in International Relations: Essays by Philip Windsor*, on which this discussion also draws.[5] Anyway, both of these volumes were published posthumously, which affords the contents a certain finality.

At the same time, reference must be made to his earlier work in order to discern a pattern of thought, if possible. His earliest work was on post-war Germany, in which he had an abiding interest from the time of his studies in Berlin in 1959-60.[6] Other early work was on arms control and détente.[7] Later his interests extended to cover other areas of the world, from the Middle East to the Far East, and he wrote more frequently on political thought and

key concepts.[8] There was timely work on particular
international crises and the European situation
throughout. He was 'in early' on several larger projects,
typically by popular demand, such as his involvement
with the Institute for Strategic Studies, later called the
International Institute for Strategic Studies (IISS), where
he was a research associate in the early sixties.[9] He was a
founding member of the editorial board of the journal
Foreign Policy, and contributor to the first issues of
Millennium: Journal of International Studies and the *British
Journal of International Studies*. That some of his writings
can also be found in rather more obscure places was
partly a result of the popular demand for his insights, but
also of his willingness to engage and participate in the
discourse wherever it was taking place—no *prima donna*,
he (though, having an eye for precision, he would no
doubt have noted the gender specific nature of that
reference).

A Journey Towards Truth and Meaning

Certainly, the subject matter of his work reflects the times
in which it was written. However, in *Strategic Thinking*
Windsor is at pains to point out the abnormality of the
nuclear age (and the 'autonomy of strategy' which it
engendered) and invokes the long historical
view—typically, he saw even this biggest of issues in a
broader context. He is also sensitive to the many local
issues which strategic thought did not (or could not)
address. There was always a wider rationale behind his
choice of subject. For example, his interest in Eastern
Europe rests on differences that gave it a unique political
context—difference in ideology, in conduct, and in
geopolitical circumstance:

> Latin America is not anybody's hostage to anything;
> Eastern Europe *is* a hostage to other considerations,
> including Western European values. In this way, the

position of Eastern Europe is radically different from that
of Latin America.[10]

Whether there is a distinction to be made between his
early work and his mature thought seems an open
question to me. Perhaps it was more a matter of a journey
towards truth (small 't') or meaning, always taking the
same general direction if following a number of different
paths. Of these two categories he has a somewhat
melancholy view:

> Truth, if not exiled from the kingdom altogether, is at least
> confined to the borders. That is, truth can only be
> apperceived at the point where the social framework
> meets other considerations: either, those of science or else
> those of an immanence which is clearly seen to depend on
> sheer faith, not on revelation or on Natural law. And,
> second, what of meaning? Meaning too has lost its
> meaning. The constant process of discovering that *we are
> other*, the constant becoming in which we are caught up, is
> bound to invalidate the individual perception of the world
> and the individual ability to act out oneself in the
> world—the ability, as it were, to create a nexus of
> meaning between individual significance and social
> significance—which had characterised the earlier attempts
> to allow Meaning to take the place of Truth.[11]

Certainly, it would have been nice to have had a final
opus magnum, but that was not his way of doing things.
The somewhat eclectic, perhaps idiosyncratic, nature of
his concerns and writings and a surprisingly broad
competence in philosophy and social sciences, in spite of
a titular specialism in strategic studies and a focus on 'the
international', makes it difficult to map or categorise his
thinking. However, from beginning to end his work was
fundamentally concerned with values, and the
difficulties, tragedies and paradoxes entailed in their
realisation. This is part of his concern with war and
strategy, since 'the articulation and realisation of values
have always been accompanied by war or the threat of
war', which, he points out, is not the same thing as saying

that all wars are about values.[12] He is concerned not to conflate (empirical) norms and values, in part because there is greater consensus on ultimate values than on contingent behavioural practices:

> And that is exactly the concern of toleration: never to lose respect for the values but to be vigilant about the norms which are deemed to be their expression.[13]

This regard for values is reflected in the element of decency to which he refers at the end of a chapter on the rationality and ethics of nuclear deterrence; neither apply in this case, as it happens: 'The very nature of that threat ultimately destroys everything that is meant by the word "decency"'.[14]

Decency was as much a personal benchmark as a public aspiration, even if this was typically presented in teasingly dismissive fashion as being the concern of the well-intentioned but naive. His observation, at the end of *Strategic Thinking*, that strategic thinking requires a sense of tragedy, also underlined by the persistent conflict of values, simply reinforces his general view—perhaps the defining character of his work—that it is difficult to be decent, and that we ought to exercise great care in our thinking about, and practice of, human affairs if we are to have any hope of recovering humanity.

A Perspective on International Relations

Windsor's work consistently challenges assumptions, and consistently does so by carefully working out how they came in to begin with, the consequences of leaving them unchallenged, and what, if anything, could be done to shake them out of our thinking. Among these assumptions are those related to positivism, and though he could pass muster as a post-positivist, since he did so before it was fashionable and while positivism still had a firm grip on the field—he might say it still does—it might be better to think of him as a pre-positivist. This critical, not to say 'Critical', orientation—though he might have accepted that label—is part of what makes it difficult to pigeonhole his position. He might also be thought of as a 'post-Liberal', given his concern with the mixed record of the liberal tradition in the 20th century. Anyway, he was never a 'Liberal' of the kind so derided by Washington conservatives and cold warriors—he took a consistently firm view of the Soviet state as 'a moral desert'[15]—and he was certainly never a reactionary as his frequent cautionary tales make clear. Indeed, it is probably correct to say that he never intended to take 'a' position and instead simply considered himself engaged in a humane undertaking—specifically, a discourse.

He has many useful things to say about methodology, epistemology and ontology, but not usually for their own sake so much as by way of elucidating political problems that rested to some degree on misunderstandings at these various levels. Otherwise he was not inclined to engage in disciplinary debates *per se*: 'The endless, and endlessly tiresome, paradigm debates seem to be pretty well over'.[16] His critique of positivism is a good example of this attitude, as it is of his critical style:

> So what on earth (or anywhere else) are the 'facts'? In brief, empirical observation which makes no attempt to establish the interpretative framework within which facts can be said to exist and have a meaning is condemned to the random. Natural scientists are perfectly aware of this. It is their country cousins, the social scientists, who are reluctant to see it.[17]

His tendency to keep even abstract insights grounded in practical considerations is also evident in methodological observations:

> To go on saying 'deterrence works' is to make a statement that is either meaningless when not circular, or else that invites experimental challenge. According to the principles of philosopher of science Sir Karl Popper, a general statement of that order must be capable of refutation if it is to have any meaning. Unfortunately there

is only one way of testing the statement, and if experiment then refuted it, few would live to tell the tale. It is safer as well as more logical to regard it as meaningless.[18]

In all this is an indication of Windsor's view of the 'discipline' and of the subject matter: that a thorough grounding in the facts is a necessary but insufficient condition of knowledge, and that ideas provide the framework of meaning.

What seems generally to be agreed by his students, colleagues, readers and interlocutors is that he was both wise and brilliant (something he often said of others whose thinking impressed him, but did not seem to be aware of in himself). This view is reinforced by one of the features of his thinking, particularly visible in retrospect: its apparent prescience. The 'post-conflict' situation in Iraq, the continuing Israel-Palestine conflict, and the 'War on Terror', which currently preoccupy media and policy circles, are issues on which Windsor's views would have been highly valued (as they were on current affairs during his lifetime), but in fact they are to be found in his extant work over many years. The last paragraph of 'Terrorism and International Order', for example, points out the risk to legitimacy, and the need for patience: 'Discretion and containment are the watchwords, not demonstrations of strength and resolve'.[19] Windsor gave considerable thought to the phenomenon of terrorism, and his insights hold true: 'Terrorism expresses a situation in which the conditions of a historical legacy have created a cause that can no longer be defined in terms of political compromise but instead must be redefined in terms of a moral claim'.[20]

In the conclusions of *Strategic Thinking* concerning the post-Cold War condition he identifies the unwarranted optimism of strategic thought and expectations of a new order, when in fact it is necessary to start 'with the assumption not that war is abnormal but that peace is difficult to achieve'.[21] Other indications of prescience are evident in earlier works, such as a book on *German*

Reunification written not in 1990, but in 1969; of course, the context was quite different but the apparent prescience here, as in his other work, lies not in privileged access to a crystal ball—prediction was not his game—but in his understanding attitude and sensitive approach to the subject matter: in this case, concern with 'the meaning of reunification', and the observations that 'the German problem was inherently transitional' and that 'time' was a factor.[22]

Crises in international relations always provide rich pickings for the careful scholarly observer, and Windsor makes good use of such opportunities. Naturally, some of the impetus for this was the demand for timely policy-relevant insights on current affairs, as in the case of *IISS Adelphi Papers* as well as briefings to military and policy-making audiences and to the media. However, Windsor's approach to crisis is as circumspect as it is to on-going systemic issues, and while there is always a thorough command of the detailed facts, it is never reportage. His first work, ostensibly a history of post-war Berlin, is actually a much broader disquisition on European security, Cold War politics and 'the setting of international relations' that he saw reflected in (and engendered by) the Berlin crises. This book includes a treatment of local politics in the city, which typifies, and perhaps formed the basis for, his appreciation of the connection between local and wider events. Illustratively, he cites Otto Suhr's remark of December 1956:

> Berlin's history . . . showed a small community struggling for freedom and autonomy, yet signified a decisive phase of the Cold War between the two power blocs.[23]

Writing on 'NATO and the Cyprus Crisis' in 1964, he skilfully lays out the background context—noting, for example, that British efforts to ensure stability 'have ended by extending the scope of a colonial conflict from one government to three'.[24] He is also sensitive enough to look at the issue from the differing perspectives of key players (as under the headings 'Seen from Athens' and 'Seen from Ankara'), and leads off the closing section with the rather quaint question 'What is the moral of this story?'. He then proceeds to answer this apparently innocent question with typical insight and prescience by drawing out implications that go far beyond the immediate crisis: 'NATO', he concludes,

> could achieve much by timely and preventative diplomacy. This might, indeed, prove to be one of its chief functions if it is to evolve and deal with the political problems of coordination and control which its military policies are likely to impose.[25]

That we can see the merits of this advice in current circumstances is testimony to his long view of immediate and contingent events.

In his treatment of the impact of the crises of 1980 (Iran and Afghanistan) he focuses on the implications for the Atlantic Alliance (differing European and American views in turn generating a third crisis, within the Alliance itself), and specifically Germany's pivotal role.[26] In so doing, he takes the particulars of political crises (limited in time and space), shows how they precipitate a more troubling systemic crisis and maps the implications for the future. Thus Windsor examines the broader issues flushed out by catalytic events, using the crises as a fulcrum for his analysis rather than assuming some meaning in the uninterpreted facts or chronology of events.

Following the Soviet invasion of Czechoslovakia, Windsor, with his co-author Adam Roberts, quickly produced an excellent book,[27] which his former colleague James Mayall describes as:

> perhaps the best illustration of his approach to the study of politics. Three qualities in particular stand out—a passionate engagement with his subject matter, an intuitive empathy with those who lived 'on the edge' and whose struggle for freedom had necessarily to be conducted within the constraints imposed on them by

history, and a belief none the less that it is ultimately ideas that shape events.[28]

On the central issue of war, and Windsor's interest only arises from the centrality of the issue and its changing nature, he notes 'that while war continues, it will increasingly become the enemy of the state rather than its servant, and a threat to civil society rather than its protector'.[29] Of guerilla war he states: 'It is the armed expression of the crisis of modernisation in traditional society'.[30] His keen interest in strategic issues and the prospects for controlling war seems to be accompanied by an underlying frustration:

> wars fought in areas or over issues that are remote from the global context of superpower interaction and the risk of nuclear escalation need not be limited at all: the participants can use all means available to massacre each other indefinitely.[31]

Such subtlety of judgment, always supported by huge reserves of knowledge and sensitive observational insight, and all clearly stated, are the hallmarks of his work.

Consistently prescient, he left us with some useful guidance for the future: 'The role of the superpower has vanished, and no actor can possibly hope to fill it'.[32] He also suggests that Mao rejected such a role for China, if it were available, having observed the difficulties faced by the Soviet Union and the United States.[33] This observation that the role has now vanished stands against a prevailing assumption that there is one superpower left, which now has a unique responsibility for bringing order to the world. Of course the United States may well have such a responsibility, but it is one which is ultimately shared even by those states, nations, groups, individuals and organisations which have little power to influence affairs. Windsor was quite clear about the dangers of thinking otherwise, outside of an internationalist framework, and also of assuming universals about people. He notes the risk of falling into 'the monstrous anti-human heresy of regarding one culture as humanly superior to another, instead of culturally more promising'. Even when 'it is necessary to support cultures of humane and democratic value', this brings with it a 'moral debt' owed to the people who lose out when policy choices favour one side over another.[34] Foreign policy can promote universalist ideas, but only through internationalist practice.

His views on the role of the United States in the world written 30 years ago seem to fit the current circumstances like a glove:

> What I am therefore suggesting is that one of the obligations of a powerful democratic state in a period when the state system needs to be augmented by a real international system is not to arrogate to itself, as a state, the right to intervene in those areas where the international borders on the universal, but to strengthen or create those international agencies, those supranational commissions, those standing conferences, which might be able to work towards a genuinely universal code.[35]

As to the discipline, or perhaps meeting point, of International Relations, he clearly thought it important enough to dedicate his life to understanding better—and he never confused its importance with his own. He suggested that it 'has superseded previous endeavours in political philosophy because it is concerned with the survival of humanity as they were not';[36] not many are as well placed to make such a statement with casual confidence. 'But to supersede is not to transcend . . . ', and so he refers to a discourse that 'takes place where other disciplines meet', 'concerned with the relationship between knowledge and social relations'.[37] This last observation is consistent with his more particular conclusion about the future of strategic thinking which invokes an alternative disciplinary orientation of 'international sociology' and suggests that this provides 'a better prospect than most for dealing with the conflicts that arise from the democratization of international society'.[38]

All this would be enough of a legacy for most, but there is more in the detail of each piece of work, in the asides and the interpretations.

A Manner of Speaking

Windsor's style, which varies according to purpose (or whim), is always tied up with clear delivery of the serious content, and some of the presentational genius of his lecturing comes through in the writing, as does the occasional element of wit to elevate a potentially dry topic. Commenting on the preponderance of conventional forces on the Soviet side, he quotes Marilyn Monroe: '"You've got to make the most of what you've got". And what they had were enormous land and air forces in western Russia and Eastern Europe'.[39] At times there are satirical statements, which are then quickly turned to good critical purposes: 'If only the feminine values could supersede the masculine, the world would be at peace: "Have a nice epoch, now!"'.[40]

There is eloquent praise for those thinkers he takes seriously: 'From the near-desert of the preceding discourse, Clausewitz's work emerges like a torrential river'. He also has great respect for Raymond Aron, an interpreter of Clausewitz.[41] 'Hegel, in the development of a complex, and indeed omniscient, philosophy of the mind and spirit, implied a revolution in the consciousness of history and also a revolution in the consciousness of consciousness'. He makes good, though critically aware, use of Hegelian categories.[42] Few others understood (and applied) these thinkers as well. There is guarded praise also for some practitioners:

> Brandt was emerging as a prominent pragmatic radical, dedicated more to organisation than ideology, and consciously attempting to adapt his organisation to the

straitened circumstances of post-war Europe: a man of the same company as Gaitskell or Kreisky.[43]

He also has criticism for some where the circumstances warrant it, but these were usually practitioners and the wry insights provide an entertaining commentary on the politics of the day (he was slower to criticise anyone making a serious effort to struggle with important problems): Curtis LeMay ' . . . whose approach to strategy might be summed up as "Aw, Hell, let's drop it"';[44] 'John F. Kennedy's mendacious election cries about a "missile gap"';[45] 'Barbara Castle and her like end by turning the welfare state into a form of tyranny';[46] Henry Kissinger 'is, it seems to me, a conservative who has not troubled to spell out his philosophy or his history . . . '.[47] In making these jibes at practitioners, he was also aware that they were not necessarily engaged in his own philosophical project—even if he wished they were, to some extent at least: ' . . . foreign policy is made by practitioners, and no carpenter ever made a table by reading Plato'.[48]

Where others might cite their academic colleagues for insight or support, Windsor looks more widely for his points of reference—and makes sparse use of footnotes, being a font of first-hand knowledge and having confidence in his arguments. In briefly surveying reactions to Napoleon, he refers in a single opening paragraph to Beethoven (destroyed dedication), Hegel (exulted), Wordsworth (grieved), Tolstoy (made fun), and most poignantly, an anonymous Belgian peasant: 'If that man's face was a clock, no one would dare look at it to tell the time'.[49] The depth of his understanding rests on extensive reading and wide interests: in writing on the justification of the state, he refers to Dante, Dostoyevsky, Galileo, Goethe, Hegel, Jung, Newton, Popper, Skinner and Wittgenstein, among others—and manages to do so without 'name dropping'. In the same piece of work, he goes on to note that,

It is surely striking that the foundation of the Society for
the Abolition of the Slave Trade, Mary Wollstonecraft's
Vindication of the Rights of Women, and Babeuf's *Conspiracy
of the Equals* all occur within ten years of each other. In
historical terms, these movements of thought can be said
to have been simultaneous. And the components of all
three—race, sex and class—haunt the political and social
thinking of the modern world.[50]

A Legacy

The habit of translating particulars into a comprehensible
philosophical and historical account of intellectual and
political practices is one of the most useful characteristics
of Windsor's work—he berates Kissinger for not doing
the same. His readers and listeners will perhaps recall
their ears pricking up whenever he prefaced a remark
with 'in historical terms' or 'in philosophical terms'. His
characterisation of the problems of the 20th century, for
example, is in terms of the unrecognised distinctions
between 'the noumenal' (timeless essence) and 'the
phenomenal' (temporal appearance), and between
common humanity and collective humanity, which made
that century discontinuous with itself—and he can (and
does) slot a raft of particulars into that scheme.[51] So it is
that he identifies the larger problems of
knowledge—something of an antidote, given his
criticisms of behaviourism and empiricism:

> The main problem for anyone concerned with the
> questions of political order and the articulations of moral
> choice (and the world teems with such questions) is how
> to devise a language in which these questions find their
> context.[52]

He suggests an approach to this problem, which begins
by considering the state as a self-regarding entity, and
ends with the possibility of criticism and change in
societies, in which 'states can be judged, condemned and
encouraged by the common understanding of the human

mind; and in which humans can become more than themselves'.[53]

Those potent characteristics of his work that might be identified as instinct, intuition, inspiration or imagination suggest a kind of spiritual awareness that is not made explicit. The inclination to view events in their holistic context, and to distinguish between noumena and phenomena, suggests one whose mind inclines to the 'right hemisphere' and has the 'left hemisphere' rational ordering of sensory perception firmly under the control of this wider understanding of the essence of things.

Not all of Windsor's legacy is in written form. One of the greatest intellectual pleasures was attending a series of seminars he organised at the LSE entitled 'Political Questions in the Philosophical Context' which seemed to be attended by a self-selected group, the selection being predicated largely on his presence and the prospect of a few thorny gems of insoluble problems—for which he inevitably had some sort of solution. It is instructive that among those associated with these seminars were respected colleagues from other departments, and disciplines: for example, a leading sociologist (Donald Macrae) and social psychologist (Roger Holmes). Students also enjoyed the intellectual pleasures afforded by his lectures (always a stimulating *tour de force*) and teaching seminars. In this context as in others he was often generous with his students (not that he had time, or patience, for everyone), and would always give credit where due, for example by citing and acknowledging some of his cleverest students when their insights were useful to the project at hand (e.g., Rebecca Grant, on Eisenhower; Hayo Krombach, on Hegel; Leon Mangasarian and Spyros Economides, for help with *Strategic Thinking*).

A Life's Work

Of the man himself, for all the profundity of his thought and the seriousness of his subject matter, he had a light touch that shows up both in the style of his work, and in many of his personal exchanges. It is suggested above that there was an ego to reckon with in Windsor, but it was not of the usual sort found in the rare atmosphere of academic reputations: there was a conscious orientation towards the transcendent mind and spirit, and this brings with it a certain self-awareness—'one can't transcend oneself'. Certainly he was a conscious, and humble, participant in the global discourse which he struggled to explain, understand and improve—for him it is, essentially, a discourse about human consciousness. He was not an existentialist, but he appreciated the nature of individual responsibility in wider events. He had concern for the less advantaged both personally and in his thinking about the more marginal areas of international relations—perhaps something to do with not being of great physical stature, or particularly good health; perhaps to do with being born in pre-independence India (New Delhi, 1935) and being witness to the human consequences of world events until the end of the century and his life (London, 2000).

In some respects Windsor might be characterised as a radical, in the English tradition (which is not to say eccentric). In a broadcast in 1969 he lamented the corruption of the tradition of radical dissent which had once been concerned with improving the world.[54] To avoid the impression of hagiography, it should also be said that he was a man for all that and had his share of problems. Nevertheless, he also had a sharp and broad sense of humour and his diminutive form often emitted a deeply toned and engaging chuckle. There was also an accepting demeanour which seemed to be related to those characteristics of mind mentioned above. I recall a teasing, and telling, reference to him as a Yoda-like character—the sort of reference to popular culture he would have enjoyed. It might be said that he deserves the same accolade that one reviewer gave his last book: 'a minor classic'.[55]

It is difficult to separate a person from their life's work, and so it is that much of Windsor's character is tied up in his intellectual concerns. His own predicament belongs to us all, and he is 'tempted at the end to quote one last philosopher: '"What" asked Friedrich Nietzsche, "might yet be made of Man?"'.[56] Precisely because such questions are concerned with the interpretation of becoming, 'the readaptation of norms and values will continue to be painful'.[57] And so it is that our struggle to achieve decency in human relations is bound to involve tragedy along the way, as it did for him.

While *Strategic Thinking*, his last book, surveys the sequential attempts to control war by moral, then legal, then political means, and finally describes the peculiar reversal of that Clausewitzian relationship in the nuclear age (when strategy determined politics), the book is also a 'farewell' to the nuclear age and its modes of thought, because of their 'increasing irrelevance . . . to the causes of conflict and of peace in the contemporary world'.[58]

As it turned out, this was also a personal farewell, and Philip Windsor's legacy is thus a programme of work for the rest of us: 'It is an imperative requirement to bring peace under control . . . But the abnormality of peace still needs a framework of thought'.[59] In showing us how to think about international relations in terms other than those of its own limited discourse, which are typically self-referential, and in invoking broader categories of thought on 'the tragic nature of human existence in international society',[60] he has also given us the tools to do the work. 'Not a bad vineyard to toil in, after all . . . '.[61]

References

1. Philip Windsor, 'Cultural Dialogue in Human Rights', in *The End of the Century: The Future in the Past*, eds. Nobutoshi Hagihara, Akira Iriye, Georges Nivat, and Philip Windsor (Tokyo: Kodansha International, 1995) and Philip Windsor, *Studies in International Relations: Essays by Philip Windsor*, ed. Mats Berdal (Brighton: Sussex Academic Press, 2002), 90. Citations from this collection note the original sources, but refer to the page number in this volume.
2. Philip Windsor, *Strategic Thinking: An Introduction and Farewell*, eds. Mats Berdal and Spyros Economides (London: Lynne Rienner, 2002), 181.
3. Ibid.
4. Windsor, 'Cultural Dialogue in Human Rights'; Windsor, *Studies in International Relations*, 77-90. This paper was given at a General Seminar of the LSE's International Relations Department, and Windsor attached some importance to its content.
5. Windsor, *Studies in International Relations*.
6. Philip Windsor, *City on Leave: A History of Berlin, 1945-1962* (London: Chatto and Windus, 1963).
7. Alastair Buchan and Philip Windsor, *Arms and Stability in Europe* (London: Chatto and Windus, 1963) and Philip Windsor, *Germany and the Management of Détente* (London: Chatto and Windus, 1971).
8. For example, Philip Windsor, 'The Evolution of the Concept of Security in International Relations', in *New Perspectives on Security*, ed. Michael Clarke (London: Brassey's Ltd., 1993), 61-70. This book is based on Lectures given at the Centre for Defence Studies, London.

9. Windsor's second book, *Arms and Stability in Europe*, was co-authored with IISS's first director, Alastair Buchan.
10. Philip Windsor, 'Superpower Intervention', in *Intervention in World Politics*, ed. Hedley Bull (Oxford: Clarendon Press, 1984); Windsor, *Studies in International Relations*, 216.
11. Philip Windsor, 'The Justification of the State', in *The Reason of States: A Study in International Relations Theory*, ed. Michael Donelan (London: Allen and Unwin, 1978); Windsor, *Studies in International Relations*, 29-30.
12. Windsor, *Strategic Thinking*, 178.
13. Windsor, 'Cultural Dialogue in Human Rights'; Windsor, *Studies in International Relations*, 87.
14. Windsor, *Strategic Thinking*, 165.
15. Philip Windsor, 'America's Moral Confusion: Separating the Should from the Good', *Foreign Policy* 13, Winter (1973/74); Windsor, *Studies in International Relations*, 184.
16. Philip Windsor, 'Foreword', in *The Study of International Relations: The State of the Art*, eds. Hugh C. Dyer and Leon Mangasarian (London: Macmillan, 1989); Windsor, *Studies in International Relations*, 18.
17. Windsor, 'The Justification of the State'; Windsor, *Studies in International Relations*, 31.
18. Windsor, *Strategic Thinking*, 161.
19. Philip Windsor, 'Terrorism and International Order', *Atlantic Community Quarterly* 25, Summer (1987); Windsor, *Studies in International Relations*, 200.
20. Ibid., 195.
21. Windsor, *Strategic Thinking*, 181.
22. Philip Windsor, *German Reunification* (London: Elek Books, 1969).
23. Windsor, *City on Leave*, 162.

24. Philip Windsor, 'NATO and the Cyprus Crisis', *Adelphi Papers*, no. 14 (London: IISS, 1964), 3.
25. Ibid., 16.
26. Philip Windsor, 'Germany and the Western Alliance: Lessons from the 1980 Crises', *Adelphi Papers*, no. 170 (London: IISS, 1981).
27. Philip Windsor and Adam Roberts, *Czechoslovakia 1968: Reform, Repression and Resistance* (London: Chatto and Windus, 1969).
28. James Mayall in an Obituary, *The Independent*, 15 July 2000.
29. Philip Windsor, 'The State and War', in *The Condition of States*, ed. Cornelia Navari (Milton Keynes: Open University Press, 1991), 141.
30. Windsor, *Strategic Thinking*, 154.
31. Ibid., 140.
32. Windsor, *Strategic Thinking*, 172.
33. Windsor, 'Superpower Intervention'; Windsor, *Studies in International Relations*, 216.
34. Windsor, 'America's Moral Confusion'; Windsor, *Studies in International Relations*, 191.
35. Ibid., 192.
36. Windsor, 'Foreword'; Windsor, *Studies in International Relations*, 19-20.
37. Ibid.
38. Windsor, *Strategic Thinking*, 181.
39. Ibid., 56.
40. Philip Windsor, 'Women and International Relations: What's the Problem?', *Millennium: Journal of International Studies* 17, no. 3 (1988); Windsor, *Studies in International Relations*, 217.
41. Windsor, *Strategic Thinking*, 24.
42. Windsor, 'The Justification of the State'; Windsor, *Studies in International Relations*, 29.
43. Windsor, *City on Leave*, 176.
44. Windsor, *Strategic Thinking*, 55.

45. Ibid., 57.
46. Windsor, 'The Justification of the State'; Windsor, *Studies in International Relations*, 25.
47. Philip Windsor, 'Henry Kissinger's Scholarly Contribution', *British Journal of International Studies* 1, no. 1 (1975); Windsor, *Studies in International Relations*, 240.
48. Windsor, 'America's Moral Confusion'; Windsor, *Studies in International Relations*, 189.
49. Philip Windsor, 'The Clock, the Context and Clausewitz', *Millennium: Journal of International Studies* 6, no. 2 (1977); Windsor, *Studies in International Relations*, 134.
50. Windsor, 'The Justification of the State'; Windsor, *Studies in International Relations*, 26.
51. Philip Windsor, 'The Twentieth Century as Self-Conscious History', in *The End of the Century: The Future in the Past*, eds. Nobutoshi Hagihara, Akira Iriye, Georges Nivat, and Philip Windsor (Tokyo: Tokyo University Press, 1985); Windsor, *Studies in International Relations*, 46-47.
52. Windsor, 'The Justification of the State'; Windsor, *Studies in International Relations*, 36.
53. Ibid., 41.
54. This information is from an Obituary by his former student and co-author Adam Roberts, *The Guardian*, 24 June 2000; its appearance in this particular organ is something of an irony given Windsor's taunting remark about 'the confused admiration [of] *Guardian* liberals, and the bright-eyed radicals' in 'The Justification of the State', 37.
55. Michael Howard, Review of Windsor's *Strategic Thinking*, *Survival* 44, no. 4 (2002): 173-74.
56. Windsor, 'Cultural Dialogue in Human Rights'; Windsor, *Studies in International Relations*, 90.
57. Ibid., 87.

58. Windsor, *Strategic Thinking*, 170.
59. Ibid., 179, 180.
60. Ibid., 181.
61. From the concluding sentence of Windsor, 'Foreword'; Windsor, *Studies in International Relations*, 19-20.

Pragmatism and International Relations in the Age of Banker's Capitalism: Susan Strange's Vision for a Critical International Political Economy[*]

Ronen Palan

Susan Strange should not have made it into this book. This is not meant to be a comment on the quality of her thought. On the contrary, elsewhere I have argued that Susan Strange was one of the most innovative and influential International Relations (IR) theorists.[1] It is a comment on the *type* of IR and International Political Economy (IPE) she sought to establish. If the truth is to be told, like many of those who are considered at the top of their disciplines, Susan Strange was an empire builder, but she was an empire builder of the wrong kind: impatient, unsystematic and most importantly, she never developed a unifying theory of political economy. Lacking an over-arching theory, she ended up advancing many theories. Indeed, she seemed to have lost confidence in the possibility of a general theory

[*] I thank Christopher May and Stefano Guzzini for great many helpful comments they have made on an earlier draft of this paper.

altogether and tried to construct her empire of IPE on shifting sands—literally. She tried to institutionalise change as a foundation of a discipline; but what are the prospects for such an approach in the long term?

I do not want to turn this contribution into a personal tribute to Susan Strange. There is no greater injustice to her than a long-winded appreciation consisting ultimately of empty words. I would like to continue here, in her spirit and through her work, an exploration of a theme, an obsession even, that occupied her throughout her life: the quest for a distinct 'discipline' of IR that recognises, first, the powerful and decisive influence the capitalist system exerts on contemporary international affairs, and second, that contemporary capitalism is distinctly different from 19th century's industrial capitalism. I advance here a paradoxical argument. On the one hand, this text can be read as an analysis of a failure, Susan Strange's failure to establish the foundations of such a discipline.[2] On the other hand, despite appearances, there was a great coherency and consistency to her thought. Her ideas were misunderstood, I believe, because they went counter to the familiar traditions of political economy: classical political economy, neo-classical economics and Marxist political economy. Having dispensed with IR theory, and having failed to identify a distinct school of political economy to draw upon, it appeared that Susan Strange had no theory at all. This is incorrect. Through her keen powers of observation and meticulous research, she constructed a distinct picture of modern capitalism, and had strong and coherent views of the role of IPE in analysing it.[3] The picture she came up with, I argue, is quite unique, but not entirely so. In fact, her attitude and methodology bears great resemblance to certain strands of pragmatic philosophy, and more interestingly, her concept of political economy contains certain notions that are similar to the pragmatic political economy of Thorstein Veblen and John Commons. I view Susan

Strange, therefore, as an evolutionary economist of a kind, and a theorist who was not entirely aware of the tradition of thought that most closely corresponded to her ideas.

I.

Strange was unconventional in many ways. But one of the more surprising elements in her thought, and the one that gives us an insight into her project, was the peculiar way she treated the historiography of IR: for Susan Strange, it appears, the discipline of IR was devoid of history! She was aware of course of the conventional or 'official' history of IR, spanning allegedly from Thucydides to Machiavelli, Hobbes, Rousseau and Morgenthau. But she treated this history with derision. The alternative history—from Vico, Gramsci, Polanyi to Foucault—fared no better. When asked who she drew inspiration from, she responded invariably that she was either resolutely 'eclectic' or would mention few close acquaintances, slightly older than her. Often these 'greats' appeared to have been picked at random, someone she has read in her latest book, a discussion she has had with somebody an hour ago. . . . Such cavalier attitude to the great traditions of thought in the social sciences and IR was interpreted by some to mean that she had no concern for philosophy or methodology, and that she was little more than a shrewd and knowledgeable commentator. This is a mistake. Anyone who had come across her personal library, now placed at Nottingham Trent University, would know that she was a voracious reader of philosophy, political economy and comparative politics. There must have been deeper reasons, I believe, for her rejection of conventional historiography of IR.

Her rejection goes, in fact, to the heart of the problem she had with IR as a discipline, and, more broadly, with the politics of disciplines: how they emerge, how they 'muscle in' on neighbouring disciplines, and how they assert themselves in that permissive environment in which analytical and policy making theories get confused. Theorising, after all, is not something innate that we are born with; we are conditioned to think of theory, and of the nature of theorising, from what passed before us. Theorising is another instance of habitual thinking; we are socialised into believing that a particular academic way is the correct way—or, to use a fashionable institutionalist language: 'we learn by doing'. Not surprisingly, the more successful models of theory making in the social sciences derive from the sciences. In that sense, we are all would-be scientists; only the different traditions of the social sciences and humanities diverge in their interpretation of the scientific method and its applicability to social and human affairs. Notwithstanding the long tradition of thought critical of the shallow application of Newtonian mechanics to the social sciences, from Dilthey, Rickert, through Heidegger, Weber up to Feyerabend and Sayer, an attitude that had become almost universal is to equate theory with what Pierce describes as 'pure theory'.[4]

Pure theory can be seen simply as those theories that begin from general principles that are taken for granted. Whether the theoreticians are aware of it or not, theory in this case is the process of working out these prior assumptions logically. Although theory often presents itself as a series of generalisations and abstractions, a distillation of the 'world out there', pure theory can be recognised in that it describes a world bounded by an if-then proposition.[5] Kenneth Waltz, for instance, is particularly good at developing pure theories of this nature, so is Robert Cox and Robert Gilpin. Waltz' assertion that 'the survival motive [of the state] is taken as the ground of action in a world' is such an if-then proposition.[6] For although presented as theory of international relations, Waltz theory at best tells us how international relations should work out *if and only if* all states possessed at the very least a survival motive. Therefore, the theory at best describes situations that conform to this constitutive 'if'.

Waltz, of course, is only an example of a general trend towards pure theorising. So when IPE began to forge a path for itself, people were naturally anticipating a new pure theory approach to international relations, and Susan Strange was clearly one of the leading candidates to provide us with one. But when her theory was published, it was odd theory in many ways. In *States and Markets*, Strange tried to identify the general principles that structure the international political economy. There we encounter, between the eggs and the omelette, something approaching a pure theory: the famous four structures of international political economy —production, finance, security and the knowledge structure. Not surprisingly, students were keenly interested in them. The four structures appear, on the face of it, as universals, suitable for pure theory type of analysis. Alas, under close examination the four structures proved nothing of the sort. They were provisional, merely 'a way of looking at the world'. They turned out to be heuristic categories and not the sought-after general principles of pure theory.

Frustratingly, the IPE that Susan Strange was proposing was devoid of general principles; it was a mere organising framework, a heuristic typology in place of a theory. It was a description, an on-going commentary punctuated by angry exchanges with the orthodoxy: the economists, US academics, the 'English school' and the like. In fact, it appears that Susan Strange was criticising IR for its very use of pure theory. 'Some so-called theory in international studies', she said, 'merely rearranges and describes known facts as categories or in new taxonomies'.[7] If theory merely rearranges known facts, the implications must be that such theory offers no added value at all. It appears that Strange was critical of theory per se.

Why, then, was she advocating IPE in place of IR? The answer can only be understood in the context of her critique of pure theory. Her explanation for the need for IPE was characteristically pragmatic, apparently anti-theoretical: the problem, she argued, was the self-indulgent approach to theory of the different disciplines that resulted in them retiring into a self-enclosed abstract world:

> Economics . . . is about the use of scarce resources for unlimited wants . . . Politics, though, is about providing public order and public goods . . . as a consequence . . . each discipline tends to take the other for granted. Markets are studied in economics on the assumption that they are not going to be disrupted by war, revolution or other civil disorder. Government and the panoply of law and the administration of justice are taken for granted. Politics, meanwhile, assumes that the economy will continue to function reasonably smoothly.[8]

Interestingly, these are narrow and somewhat idiosyncratic definitions of economics and politics. Her concept of economics lies within the Humean tradition of theories of scarcity, combined, curiously, with what appears as a rejection of the neo-classical theory of marginal utility. For she assumes desire to be unlimited and hence renders scarcity an ontological societal problem.[9] Politics meanwhile is reduced to governance. But leaving these issues aside, her basic critique of the two disciplines appears to derive from a pragmatic position often confused for an anti-theoretical attitude. She seems to be saying that rather than begin from general principles that 'forget' something fundamental about the world, and than 'back peddle' by rearranging categories in order to get a hold on this world, it is time to go the other way around, to begin with the facts and use theories only as tools of understanding, always provisional and hence ever dispensable. This is, again, a pragmatic approach.

I use the term 'pragmatic' here for a purpose, because pragmatism is not the anti-theory that some readers may take it to be, pragmatism is a specific social philosophy that emerged primarily in the United States in the late 19th century. Pragmatism is defined by John Commons as follows: 'Pragmatic or Scientific Theorists [may be distinguished] in so far as they have an eye on the worthfulness of their reasoning for understanding, experimentation, taking chances, and guiding themselves and other participants in the future'.[10] Although I am not aware that Strange has made any references to Pierce, James or Dewey,[11] this characterisation of theory seems to me to be an apt description of Strange's approach to theory. Theory, according to the institutionalist economist John Commons, is judged by its usefulness. Does philosophical pragmatism holds the key to Susan Strange's brand of IPE? I think so.

Pragmatism is also associated with particular political economic theories of Veblen and Commons, which are neither classical nor neo-classical, nor Marxists, and which I believe share many of her observations and insights into the dynamics of modern capitalism. Indeed, variants of institutional economics (minus its militant critique of business) were currents in Business Studies, a field, I note, she was particularly interested in.

II.

There is, of course, another, more important reason for the shift from IR to IPE. The 'new International Political Economy', as Murphy and Tooze called it, advocated among others by Susan Strange, was not simply about adding a tinge of economics to a settled view of a (political) relationship between states; the new IPE sought to redefine the very foundations of IR.[12]

It is useful at this point to clarify what do I mean by 'mainstream IR', so that we understand better the nature of the critique of the new IPE. If there is a mainstream in IR, it concerns itself with the relationship between states; the latter viewed externally as unified actors. The theoretical arguments for treating the state as a unified actor may vary. Surprisingly perhaps, modern realist thought traces its origins to the counter-reformation movement, and more recently to the late 18th century idealist-romantic theory of the state.[13]

During the 19th century, the romantic-idealist movement affected an important reinterpretation of the work of Machiavelli. No longer seen as a mere cynic, Machiavelli was viewed now as the father of the science of politics. The 'realism' of Machiavelli implied that successful policy making hinges on three factors:

1) Cold, critical and accurate assessment of a political situation;

2) An element of chance—*fortuna*;

3) An element of skilled leadership—*virtú*.

These ideas had a strong current in the European history of thought, particularly in Germany and Italy where progressive nationalist and liberal thinkers were seeking the construction of a unified state. By the late 19th century, Heinrich von Treitschke incorporated Machiavelli's ideas into his organic and spiritual theory of the state.[14] Successful leadership, he argues, requires a combination of a cold assessment of the current situation with an analysis of the distribution of power. He called this policy *Realpolitik*. Hans J. Morgenthau, who was strongly influenced by the work of Treitschke and Friedrich Meinecke, dubbed his theory of international relations 'political realism', a literal translation of Treitschke's *Realpolitik*.[15]

For the German Romantics, the unitary state possessed a personality of its own. Lately, however, the state is no longer seen as possessing a personality, but is considered instead as a set of institutional structures bent on perpetuating itself. True, states are caught up in a two-level game, but they appear on the international level game as unified actors. Similarly, the more popular strand of constructivism, Wendtian constructivism, accepts the unified state theory.

In fact, state centrism, indeed nationalism, is written into the very name of our discipline: 'Inter-*national* Relations'. As its name suggests, IR is a branch of study that is founded on the belief that nations are the main actors in world politics. The modern discipline of IR emerged, therefore, not with Thucydides, nor with Westphalia, nor, I am afraid to say, in Aberystwyth; it emerged in the late 18th century at the point when nations were considered independent actors in world politics. The idea of the nation as an independent actor was not viewed as a metaphor or an analogy, but was taken very seriously. At its core was an idealist theory.[16] It is important to understand that the new IPE, led by Susan Strange, strives to move away from the idealist origins of IR, and also, and perhaps more importantly, from the nationalist perspective that still pervades the field. In that sense, the new IPE offers a real break with mainstream IR theory.

III.

Away from the profoundly 'nationalist' perspective on international affairs that mainstream IR theory is advocating, the new IPE reorients itself towards the traditions of political economy. This is somewhat ironic because it is not always appreciated that IR and political economy share the same point of origins in political philosophy. Nonetheless, modern political economy offers IPE a route out of the pervading nationalist perspective because it emerged during the pre-nationalist phase, in the mercantilist debates on the welfare of the *commonwealth.* Locke, for instance, founded his theories on the distinction between productive work—work that produces wealth for the commonwealth—and usurpation. Productive work was to be encouraged, while monopolies, at that time government's grants and special privileges which benefited individuals and not the community, were seen as unproductive. This argument became the basis of the different variants of labour theories of value in classical economics. According to the labour theory of value, value could be measured objectively in terms of the amount of 'dead labour', as Marx called it, embedded in the object. However, theories of political economy underwent two important transformations. The first saw the emergence of neo-classical economics in the later years of the 19th century. According to neo-classical economics, value ('use-value') is not embedded in the object but is subjective, a functional relationship between scarcity and desire.

The second transformation saw the rise of institutional (or evolutionary) economics, and it is the latter that corresponds most closely to Susan Strange's thought. There was a good historical reason for the close parallels between Strange and the evolutionary economists. Most of her detailed empirical research was in the area of 'finance', and I use the term in inverted commas because the conventional view of finance as a separate realm dealing with money and credit is simply false. Finance in the modern world concerns predominantly the exchange of property, or rather property titles. One of the distinguishing traits of evolutionary economics was the idea that capital itself has a history, so that the nature of capital and the capitalist system changed dramatically in the late 19th century. According to this view, Marxism froze at an early stage of capitalism. Hence, Marxists still take the view that production and finance are two separate realms. They also hold not to an incorrect, but to an anachronistic theory of capital. A later phase of capitalism saw an important transformation in the nature of property and in the relationship between finance and production, which institutionalists like Commons and Veblen called 'banker's capitalism'.

Crucial in banker's capitalism was the emergence of a new concept of property, intangible property, accepted and legitimised by the courts of the United States.[17] Let us take an example: What is, say, the value of the *Coca-Cola company, Intel, Microsoft* or *Armani*? In classical economic theory, the value of the *Armani* company consists of its corporeal and incorporeal assets: aggregation of land, machinery, the number of suits and shirts in its possession, plus debts and financial assets. The value that *Armani* adds to society is measured in terms of an aggregate dead labour. From a neo-classical, individualistic point of view, the value of *Armani* suits is likely to decline the more an individual possesses them. That may be true, but such theory gives no indication of the value of the company itself in the world. And by the same token, it gives no indication of how these different kinds of value can be traded and organised worldwide.

Today, the greatest component of *Armani*'s value, a value which for example can be expressed in its stock market price, is the value of its name, its brand, which is an 'intangible property'. Hence, the greatest asset of *Armani* is its name and logo. *Armani* keeps its 'brand value' not necessarily by 'flooding' the markets with as many suits and shirts it can sell at cost of production plus surplus value, but by creating demand for its products and yet limiting their numbers in the market.[18]

Armani does so by raising prices, placing its shops in exclusive areas, limiting the number of franchises and so on. In fact the market value, against which it can borrow money and affect other financial transactions, is not the aggregate corporeal capital of the company—machinery, stock of old and new suits and shirts, few buildings, but a *capitalisation of its expected net earning capacity*. Effectively, the value of *Armani, Coca Cola, Intel, Microsoft* and all the other names we are familiar with, including banks, pension funds, and service companies, are claims to differential marketing advantages which are estimated to provide future earnings, and *capital* therefore is the value of the anticipated future earning.[19]

In short, value has to do with ownership of tangible and intangible property. Intangible property can form money 'out of nothing' and the dominant game in town in modern capitalism is the buying and selling of intangible property. Exactly this is Strange's idea of *Other People's Money* as the dominant mode of capitalist investment. With the development of intangible property, modern business activities, which are normally mistaken for 'finance', became the business of obtaining money itself,

> or rather with obtaining various legal instruments such stocks, bonds, and checking accounts at the bank, which have the capacity of commanding commodities and labour in exchange. These legal instruments are evidences of ownership and not products of workmanship. They have no necessary connection with commodities, in fact are not commodities at all, but are legal instruments for controlling the supply of commodities.[20]

Since these legal instruments for controlling the supply of commodities and services give titleholders access to profit, these instruments can be traded, and have become in the modern world commodities in themselves—something that apparently Commons did not anticipate. The value of these commodities is measured primarily by their ability to produce future anticipated net profit. The ability of certain property titles to produce future profits depends largely on the ability, innovation and audacity of the titleholder to realise (or 'unlock') these values.

If *British Airways*, for instance, joined with *American Airline* (as it wished to do a few years ago) and would control over three quarters of the landing slots at Heathrow, then the merged company could use its monopolistic position to raise ticket prices. Since the market anticipates the monopolistic advantages of such a merger, it will reward the parties by raising their value. The new capital, capitalisation of anticipated rise in profits, can then be traded and that trading happens at the commanding height of the economy. This is the world of the big banks, corporations and funds that Susan Strange was one of the greatest and shrewdest observer and a world she hated so much. It is also a world which is missing entirely in traditional IR, rendering IR in the eyes of Susan Strange a fairly useless discipline. But it is a world that is largely missing or misunderstood by the other two great traditions of political economy, neo-classical economics and Marxist economics. Hence Susan Strange's rejection of the two.

IV.

I would like to propose here that Susan Strange's concept of IPE and its four structures is in fact a slightly idiosyncratic rendition of the dynamics of power of modern capital in the age of banker's capitalism.

Orthodox and Marxian economics is centred on 'use-value': on machines, commodities, natural resources and so on. For institutional economics this is a fundamental mistake, as 'material things come and go with a rapid turnover by depreciation, obsolescence, and consumption; but that which keeps up their renewal and increasing efficiency is the traditions, customs, and in the innovations handed down from one generation to the next in the evolving character of managerial transactions'.[21] If one wishes to argue that the value, say, of *General Motors* (GM), is the value of its land, machine tools, information technology (IT) and so on, which in Marxian economics is expressed by the concept of the 'organic composition of capital', then, today, machines, tools and IT are rendered completely obsolete, junk to be disposed of in about five years. For instance, GM's real

value is found in certain institutional knowledge and
know-how, managerial skills and corporate culture,
which is the only cumulative form of 'human capital':
habits, customs, ideas and technology. Is this a familiar
concept? Of course, it is. Is it not Susan Strange's
'knowledge structure'? At core I think it is, although the
knowledge structure is more ambiguous and amorphous
in her rendering.

But to institutional economics the knowledge structure
itself is the mere cumulative knowledge of centuries. The
key is to operationalise this knowledge. For that purpose,
Veblen identified the engineer as the key figure of
modern capitalism. 'Capital is not an accumulation of
past products of stored-up labour—these are
transitory and aimless—capital is a going plant of
industrial knowledge and experience guided by the
master-workman for the service of mankind'.[22] There is a
critical function played therefore by the engineer in
organising production. The technological knowledge of
GM, its corporate culture and its reliance on broader
societal customs and habits is not enough; GM provides a
crucial service in organising and managing societal
resources. It engineers not only cars; it engineers
production processes and indeed, it engineers itself.
Commons calls this the 'machine process':

> The 'machine process' is larger than the machine. It is a
> whole nation. It is procedure on the basis of a systematic
> knowledge of forces employed; agricultural and animal
> industries are machine process. It is larger than the single
> plant, since none of the processes are self-sufficient but the
> whole concert of industrial operations is to be taken as a
> machine process. . . . There must be adjustments within
> the plant, adjustments between plants and between
> industries, measurements of materials and appliances,
> standardised sizes, shapes, grades, gauges, not only of
> commodities and services, but also of time, place, and
> circumstance. It is a world-wide 'comprehensive, balanced
> mechanical process'.[23]

This 'machine process' is similar to Susan Strange's concept of the 'production structure'.

The machine process is so delicate, writes Commons, '[so] nicely is this process balanced that any disturbance at any point spreads quickly to other points and may bring down the entire process with idleness, waste, and hardship'.[24] Here is where IPE depart from institutional economics. Veblen and Commons point out that the role of the businessman is balancing out and organising the machine process, or rather, the role of business in destabilising and operating 'intentional incompetence' to augment profit.[25] The businessman is concerned with profit, and profit is achieved largely by destabilising, 'sabotaging' the production process. This is part of what we confusingly regard as the 'financial system'.

The other aspect is generally only alluded to in the work of institutional economics, and that, of course, is the role of the state and international institutions in regulating this delicate process. This role is translated in Strange parlance as part of her notion of the security structure. But her idea of the security structure consisted not only of the absence of war and violence, but also includes the entire political machinery and process of ensuring stable habitual conduct of society.

The commanding height of the modern economy is dominated by what Veblen called business culture, the culture of making money out of trading and exchange in property rights and capitalisation of expected earning capacity. The great tussle that is going on is not between finance capital and productive capital as Marxists claim. 'Finance' is a misnomer; the term is used in misrecognition of the nature of modern capitalism. Finance stands for business culture because, as Nitzan and Bichler say, capital in all its forms is 'finance'.[26] From that perspective the rise of the New Deal in the 1930s or Fordism—ideologically supported by the early constructivists—was a brave attempt at institutionalising change in the nature of capitalism and to shift it away from business culture towards a managerial system that privileges efficiency in production. To achieve this mammoth task, business was 'locked' by the planners of Bretton Woods to their nation-states, forced into an historical compromise with state and labour.[27] Fordism was, in other words, a societal attempt to harness civilisation to societal goals—to balance out the relationship between the engineer and business. That attempt has failed. The high priests of the failure were the central bankers and the 'Chicago Boys'. With the end of the social compromise, business culture is reasserting itself. Susan Strange analysed the failure in two of her books, *Casino Capitalism* and *Mad Money*.[28] But interestingly enough, she did not blame the rise of the financial fraction for the wracking of the Fordist social compromise—she did not recognise casino capitalism as the work of a distinct 'financial fraction'; she saw the changes more holistically as the reassertion of power by business, supported unfortunately by politicians and policy makers.

V.

You can see now why I do not like the four structures of international political economy in particular. It is a cope out! A framework instead of a theory. Frankly, I was under the impression that Susan was not too fond of her framework either. She considered the four structures at best a useful way of conversing with students about the nature of the world in the age of banker's capitalism. Why she did not draw on the existing edifice of institutional economics I do not know. You will notice that I was quoting heavily from John Commons's *Institutional Economics*, a book that was originally published in 1932, and draws heavily on Veblen's even earlier work. The reader is entitled to ask, if Susan Strange's ideas were so closely aligned with Veblen and

Commons, why has she never mentioned them? Surely, she must have known about their work.[29] But whether she knew them or not, or whether she would eventually have accepted aspects of institutional economics or not I do not know. What I do know, is that the world described by Veblen and Commons was the world that Susan Strange knew and disliked. And that knowledge, without necessarily knowing or accepting that particular theory, gave her unique power of observation and insight into the modern world, combined with a deep sense of injustice and corruption. It is not corruption in the way we understand it, but dishonesty and ruthlessness, which is the way business conducts its affairs, and which she disliked with passion. That is why she had no difficulties in treating the Mafia as business. It was not that she thought the Mafia acted like a legitimate business; rather she was convinced business used the same technique of power as the Mafia. In her later years, she was increasingly focusing on the great 'transactors' in the business world: financial operators, accountants, lawyers, land speculators, whom she rightly saw not as agents of power in the traditional sense, but as the paradigmatic types of modern capitalism.

Not surprisingly, she also possessed a deep sense of frustration with academia. The world of economists, hegemonic stability theorists, the 'English school' and the like, which she considered to be supportive either directly, or indirectly, of American hegemony by diverting attention from the real issues facing the world. But Susan was the child and in many ways the product of the 'golden age' of Fordism, she inherited a strong belief in societal power and the ability of society ameliorate the abuse of business culture. She was a constructivist in the Keynesian sense, attached to the state, not because she was 'statist' by inclination, but because she knew that the state had the powers to regulate and outlaw the worst aspects of business culture.

Although lacking a theory of capital, she nonetheless was the key inspiration for the emergence of a pragmatic, empiricist and critical school of IPE.

References

1. Ronen Palan, 'Susan Strange: A Great International Theorist', *Review of International Political Economy* 6, no. 2 (1999): 121-32.
2. Had she been with us today, I believe, the sort of failure I describe would have made her proud. The one thing Strange disliked most was the glib complacency of mainstream IR, with its derivative approaches and schools, its so-called big epistemological debates, conducted in blissful ignorance of the turmoil around us. Failure is a good thing: it means striving, open mindedness, lack of complacency and work. These are the qualities that made Susan Strange into the great force in IR she still is.
3. Most readers will be familiar with Strange's latter work, such as *Casino Capitalism* (Oxford: Blackwell, 1986); *States and Markets* (London: Pinter, 1987); and *The Retreat of the State: The Diffusion of Power in the World Economy* (Cambridge: Cambridge University Press, 1996). Innovative and powerful as they are, these works are not renown for attention to detail and meticulous empirical research. But her earlier work, such *Sterling and British Policy: A Political Study of an International Currency in Decline* (Oxford: Oxford University Press, 1971) helped establish the 'academic' credential of Strange.
4. Charles S. Pierce, 'The Fixation of Belief', *Popular Science Monthly* 12, November (1877): 1-15.
5. This is, of course, true in theory. When it comes to an examination of concrete theories we often discover that it is contestable whether they are pure or not.

6. Kenneth Waltz, *Theory of International Politics* (Reading, MA: Addison Wesley, 1979), 92.
7. Strange, *States and Markets*, 10.
8. Ibid., 14, 15.
9. This is very significant. Hume's concept of scarcity introduced ethics as an organic component of political economy. For, argued Hume, in conditions of complete abundance, there is no problem of redistribution and hence no need for ethics or justice.
10. John R. Commons, *Institutional Economics: Its Place in Political Economy* (Madison, WIS: Minnesota University Press, 1961), 102.
11. Although all three are considered the founders of pragmatism, there are many differences among them. I refer here to Pierce's variant of pragmatism.
12. Craig Murphy and Roger Tooze, eds., *The New International Political Economy* (Boulder, CA: Lynne Rienner, 1991).
13. Ronen Palan and Brook Blair, 'On the Idealist Origins of the Realist Theory of International Relations', *Review of International Studies* 19, no. 4 (1993): 385-99.
14. Heinrich von Treitschke, *Politics* (London: Constable and Co., 1916).
15. See Hans J. Morgenthau, *Politics Among Nations: The Struggle For Power and Peace* (New York: Knopf, 1948) and Friedrich Meinecke, *Machiavellism: The Doctrine of Raison d'Etat and its Place in Modern History* (London: Routledge and Kegan Paul, 1962).
16. Palan and Blair, 'On the Idealist Origins'.
17. The concept of intangible property emerged, as John Commons shows, in a serious of Court decisions in the US in the last two decades of the 19th century.
18. Commons, *Institutional Economics*, 667.
19. It may be argued that neo-classical economics is perfectly in tune with this theory of capital. That is a theoretical possibility, but due to mechanical

methodology, neo-classical economics still tries to hold on to the idea of capital 'inputs'—rendering capital instead a physical quantity. This theory was subject to a devastating critique by Piero Sraffa who demonstrated effectively how this theory is a tautology. In the words of Tabb: 'To determine the value of capital it is necessary to know the rate of interest; but to determine the rate of interest it is necessary to know the value of capital!'; William K. Tabb, *Reconstructing Political Economy: The Great Divide in Economics* (New York: Routledge, 1999), 155. For an excellent discussion, see Jonathan Nitzan and Shimshon Bichler, 'Capital Accumulation: Breaking the Dualism of "Economics" and "Politics"', in *Global Political Economy: Contemporary Theories*, ed. Ronen Palan (London: Routledge, 2000), 67-88.

20. Commons, *Institutional Economics*, 667.
21. Ibid., 660.
22. Ibid., 662.
23. Ibid., 663.
24. Ibid.
25. For an excellent discussion, see Matthew Josephson, *The Robber Barons: The Great American Capitalists, 1861-1901* (New York: Harcourt, Brace and Co., 1935).
26. Nitzan and Bichler, 'Breaking the Dualism'.
27. Eric Helleiner, *States and the Reemergence of Global Finance: From Bretton Woods to the 1990s* (Ithaca, NY: Cornell University Press, 1994).
28. Susan Strange, *Mad Money* (Manchester: Manchester University Press, 1998). See also Louis Pauly, *Who Elected the Bankers? Surveillance and Control in the World Economy* (Ithaca, NY: Cornell University Press, 1997).
29. Although according to Christopher May, a compiler of Susan Strange's bibliography, there are no

references in her work to the pragmatists and
institutional economists.

Critical Voices in a Mainstream Local: *Millennium*, the LSE International Relations Department and the Development of International Theory[*]

Mark Hoffman

For almost half of its 75 years the Department of International Relations at the LSE has played host to one of the most innovative journals in the discipline. The location of *Millennium: Journal of International Studies* within the Department is not without an element of irony. The Department's intellectual history and legacy is one that is steeped in and widely associated with the 'English School' and its account of order and justice within an anarchical society. Mainstream and traditional would not be unfounded characterisations of the outlook of the Department taken as a whole.[1] *Millennium*, on the other hand, has come to be widely associated with the more radical, dissonant, marginal, some might say wacky voices within the discipline.

What follows is a brief account of how this 'odd couple' relationship came into place and developed over

---

[*] I am grateful for comments on an earlier draft from Barry Buzan and Michael Banks.

time based on mutual support and admiration—if not always mutual understanding and comprehension. It provides some insights into the origins of the Journal and some of the key turning points in its intellectual and professional evolution. It is by no means a comprehensive account of either the Journal, the Department, the discipline or events in global politics during the period covered. Nor does it provide a detailed account or exposition of all or even most of the nearly 600 articles and 3,000-plus book reviews published in the Journal over the last 31 years. The balance of the narrative is weighted more towards the early years—a period less widely familiar to current readers of the Journal. Its tone is congratulatory, even hagiographic—but in the circumstance no apologies are offered for either of these tendencies.

In the Beginning . . .

It is worth noting the particular milieu within which *Millennium* arose as this has some bearing on its genesis, initial trajectories and the subsequent content within its pages. In the realm of international events, the US is bogged down in South East Asia, East-West relations are moving into the period of détente, the People's Republic of China is slowly opening to the West, while violent conflict convulses Northern Ireland, Nigeria, Bangladesh, and Rhodesia. Just around the corner are Watergate and Nixon's resignation, the US withdrawal from Vietnam, the October 1973 Arab-Israeli war, the subsequent oil crisis and rise of the Organisation of the Petroleum Exporting Countries (OPEC), the collapse of the Bretton Woods system and resulting Third World debt crisis.

Within International Relations (IR), the reverberations of the 'Second Great Debate', the subsequent 'post-behavioural revolution', and the theoretical and conceptual developments that would shortly coalesce into the 'inter-paradigm debate' are working their way through the discipline. On the one hand, what are now widely characterised as neo-positivist epistemologies with their associated rational-choice theories and quantitative methodologies have come to dominate the discipline in the US, leaving a small, but vocal rump group of UK-based scholars still embracing their 'classical approach' to international politics. On the other, there is the opening of disciplinary boundaries to influences from elsewhere in the social and natural sciences. Foreign Policy Analysis (FPA) and Strategic Studies have come into their own as major sub-fields, the green shoots of International Political Economy (IPE) are evident, and ecological/environmental concerns are percolating to the surface.

Outside the discipline, there are major debates and developments that would come to have a significant impact on the theoretical discourses within IR—and on the content of *Millennium*. During this formative period for the Journal there are major debates within the sociology of knowledge in light of the work of Karl Popper and Thomas Kuhn, and in sociology and philosophy over the status of positivism. Grand theory returns to political theory with the work of John Rawls, while the first intimations of the debates regarding the 'crisis of modernity' and the problems of representation are evident in strands of German and French social theorising.

It was within this international and academic environment that Professor F.S. Northedge called together a group of students in the LSE Department of International Relations to discuss the possibility of starting a new journal. Northedge felt a certain disquiet about the existing journals on offer. His view was that they were too narrow in focus (read, too US-oriented, too much concerned with current affairs at the expense of viewing contemporary problems and issues in a broader, historically informed context, and/or too beholden to the 'behaviouralists'). Northedge was also of the view that most of the major journals were too much 'in the pocket' of a small, self-selecting group of academics that only published pieces by established scholars who were more often than not in some way connected to the journals via their editorial boards. Moreover, the existing professional journals were too expensive, putting them beyond the reach of most postgraduate and research students. Quite probably preaching to the converted, Northedge argued that this situation could be corrected by offering an inexpensive, wide-ranging journal that would draw on the large pool of interesting research being carried out by research students and the younger members of the profession, particularly outside the US. Not only should the younger generation contribute scholarly pieces to the journal; Northedge felt very strongly that they should have a considerable hand in editing such a journal as well. He was equally adamant that the Department of International Relations at the LSE was fully capable of producing such a journal.

The first editorial meeting took place on 12 February 1971. It decided that the journal would be called *Millennium: Journal of International Studies*. The first part of the name was Northedge's suggestion and taken from a Tennyson poem:

> *And let*
> *thy feet, millennium hence, be set*
> *In midst of knowledge, dream'd not yet.*[2]

The latter part of the title was the product of discussion amongst the newly constituted editorial board and was intended to convey an intellectual remit beyond the narrow confines of 'international relations' and an intellectual pluralism as a sharp counter-point to the perceived intellectual and professional hegemony of the existing journals. As the then editor, Jeffrey Golden, and Northedge noted in a brief editorial in Vol. 2 No. 2, *Millennium* was intended to be a 'statement of the mutlivarious ways in which international relations are being discussed' and would be 'receptive to the value of dialogue'.

In addition to the title of the Journal, another of Fred Northedge's lasting legacies to the Journal was its distinctive logo, designed by his daughter, then a student at St. Martin's and reworked by Sylvester Bone. The distinctive 'Millennium' against a rising orb has graced the Journal's cover ever since.

While Northedge continued to provide guidance and advice to the Journal's editors and editorial board, he took a back seat and handed complete editorial control over to the students on the assumption that they would have a better sense of what were the new, cutting-edge issues in the discipline, and would be more open to publishing innovative and challenging material, both from other research students and rising stars within the academy.[3]

It is worth underscoring the students' editorial control of the Journal. While there are now several student-led and/or edited academic journals, at the time *Millennium* was unique in giving students the power to accept or reject articles for publication. In a set of processes and procedures which were put in place from the Journal's earliest days and which continue to be followed, pieces submitted to the Journal would be sent out to academic referees and then placed before the student editorial board for consideration.[4] In a deliberative and democratic process that would make Habermas smile, the editorial board meets once a week and engages in a frank, sometimes heated discussion of the merits of a particular piece and then democratically decides whether or not, and with what conditions, to accept it for publication. This editorial power is considerable, potentially idiosyncratic (given a membership that can change from week to week, let alone year to year) and has been occasionally wielded against the 'great and the good' of the discipline in a manner that has ruffled feathers and put a few egos in a state of ill temper.

Equally at variance with the practices of most academic journals whose editors were and still are appointed/anointed in something akin to a conclave of bishops electing a new Pope, all the major editorial posts of *Millennium* are democratically elected from amongst those students who take an active role in its production, with editorial teams and editorial boards often reflecting the cosmopolitan character of the LSE and IR Department student body.[5] In a further distancing from standard operating procedures, these editorial posts could only be held for a single volume. This was partly to ensure that the Journal did not come under the sway of any particular students, that its editorial stance was always fresh as each new set of editors would define the Journal's agenda for the year in which they were editing it, and partly a pragmatic response to the annual turn-over in the student membership of the editorial board. The Journal was initially produced via mimeo graphic reproduction at the LSE with secretarial support provided by the Department and the School's reprographics department printing the copies. Three issues were to be produced each year mirroring the three terms of the typical UK academic year—a quirk that continues to this day. With a print run of around a hundred, the spiral bound first issues of the Journal were sold for the princely sum of 20 pence to members of the staff at the LSE, students at the LSE (and their family and friends) and a few at other UK institutions.

The contents of these first issues were true to the initial ethos of the Journal. They included pieces by research students, some by members of staff at the LSE, a few by high profile individuals. They also covered a broad range of topics: arms control and non-proliferation, international law, the merits of Marxian-informed international theory, development issues, the politics of the United Nations (UN), Soviet foreign policy, the military-industrial complex, MNCs as international actors, the Vietnam peace agreements and the use of force in international relations.

With Vol. 3, the Journal took on a more professional feel. It moved from 'in-house' production to being properly typeset and lithographically produced by an outside printing firm. It developed a standard size and format, institutionalised an editorial house style regarding endnotes (later changed to footnotes) and *-ise* rather than *-ize* spellings.[6] Along side this improvement in its presentation, the Journal's subscription base was starting to build. The balance was still decidedly tilted towards individuals (and a consequent high turnover as a number of these were students who often did not renew their subscriptions once they left the LSE) but with a steady rise in the number of libraries taking the Journal, including those overseas. By Vol. 3, prices had doubled—to 40 pence per issue.

Consolidating an Identity: An Inter-Paradigmatic Journal

By the mid-1970s, *Millennium* had in place an underlying ethos of intellectual and academic pluralism, a functioning—if occasionally prone to crisis—editorial management and decision making process, a steadily growing subscription base and a developing reputation, both within the UK and increasingly overseas.[7] The last two elements were connected to the first. All were reflected in the Journal's self-identity that started to consolidate from Vol. 3 onwards. This, in turn, was connected to and animated by wider developments and debates within the discipline, particularly as they were reflected in the research interests of staff and especially the students in the Department.

Important in understanding this consolidation is a shift in the source and content of the academic advice and support provided to the Journal. While Northedge was a central figure in helping to establish the Journal, it was Michael Banks who came to have the more profound

impact on the intellectual and theoretical traditions that
the Journal would explore. Through his 'Concepts and
Methods of International Relations' lecture series, Banks
had become one of the main advocates of developing
theoretical positions that would constitute a counter-
weight to the intellectual and praxeological dominance of
political realism. In developing these ideas, Banks was
one of the first individuals within the discipline to latch
on to Kuhn's arguments and in particular his notion of
'paradigms' and to use this as the basis for arguing that
IR had now entered its third 'great debate'—what Banks
would famously characterise as an 'inter-paradigm
debate'.

For better or worse, these and similar ideas took hold in
the discipline. Increasingly, they also took hold among
members of the Journal's editorial board—many of whom
would have attended Banks's lectures and participated in
his seminars, not to mention taken advantage of the ease of
access to him and the length of time he was willing to
spend talking to students about international theory.

It is hardly surprising, then, that the content of the
Journal during this period broadly reflected the
contemporary academic and intellectual climate, along
side a continued engagement with contemporary issues
in world politics. Amongst a broad range of material
published, three topics or themes become prominent
within the pages of the journal: debates about
international theory itself, particularly the development
of theoretical alternatives to political realism; North-
South relations, particularly their economic dimensions;
and East-West relations.

In the realm of theory, the Journal published pieces on
the sociology of international law, the credentials and
desirability of 'sub-field dominance', the balance of power,
the scientific vs. classical approaches, and world systems
analysis. Most prominent were discussions of
interdependence, transnationalism and claims regarding an
evolving world society. The Journal's foray into these

theoretical issues is exemplified in one of the more (in)famous theoretical exchanges between James Rosenau and Fred Northedge over the importance of 'transnationalism' as a phenomenon in global politics and its implications for international theory.[8]

North-South issues came to the fore in pieces on the purpose and desirability of foreign aid, the post-73 oil crisis, the Brandt Report and the subsequent calls for a 'new international economic order', as well as contributions to the wider debates on deepening global inequalities, on development and dependency.

The third prominent topic was East-West relations in the context of the proxy wars, détente, and arms control negotiations. The Journal published pieces on the Vietnam peace agreements, the Middle East conflict, the SALT I and II negotiations, nuclear proliferation issues, tensions within the North Atlantic Treaty Organization (NATO) on its 25th anniversary, *Ostpolitik*, and US-Soviet relations. The analysis in many of these pieces reflected the optimism of the time regarding détente. All this was to change in the late 1970s and through the 1980s, as détente slowly collapsed in on itself and the 'New Right' consolidated its attacks on what it perceived as the weaknesses inherent in Western policies towards the Soviet Union. The range of these concerns/issues became the focal point for contributions to Vol. 9 No. 2—the first Special Issue of the Journal.[9]

On the back of interest in the last two themes—North-South issues and East-West tensions—*Millennium* also sought to extend its profile through the sponsorship of academic conferences and the organisation of a public lecture series. To this end, it gained funding from the Ford Foundation to mount a major conference on North-South relations in 1978. The following year it again raised funding from the Ford Foundation, this time for a conference exploring the themes of arms control and security in Europe at the beginning of what would come to be characterised as the Second Cold War. Many of the figures that participated in the conference would go on to hold important positions within the Reagan and first Bush administrations.

This was followed by other annual conferences on subjects such as Latin America and the political economy of development, East-West technology transfer, and contemporary social theory and the problem of war and peace.[10] These conferences were highly successful in raising the Journal's profile, attracting participants from the realms of academia, government and the media. In most cases, each conference resulted in an edited book that served to further enhance the Journal's prestige and raised its profile within the discipline, particularly outside the UK.[11] The costs—both financial and human—of running an annual conference, however, would soon become too high and after the 1985 conference on social theory and war and peace, the Journal stopped sponsoring a major annul conference. The tradition would be revived only from 1996, when the Journal came to celebrate its 25th anniversary.

In the late 1970s, again with a view to enhancing its profile, the Journal gained funding from Chase Manhattan bank for a series of annual public lectures to be delivered by prominent figures in the field of IR on contemporary issues. The lectures would subsequently be published in the Journal.[12] While the first two lectures by Raymond Aron and Ernest Gellner went off quite smoothly, the relationship between the Journal and the bank went down hill quite rapidly from the third lecture onwards. Delivered by Johan Galtung, he used the occasion to 'bite the hand that was feeding him' that evening. In the course of revisiting his 'structural theory of imperialism' he mounted a fierce attack on the institutions of the North and their role in the growing gap between the haves and have-nots, with Chase Manhattan bank as the whipping post for the purposes of his argument. The leading figures from the bank squirmed uncomfortably in their seats and unsurprisingly the scheduled post-lecture dinner was abruptly cancelled. Needless to say, Chase Manhattan was not best pleased. A lunch at the bank was arranged to discuss future invitations. The bank made clear its dissatisfaction and hoped the Journal would invite someone more 'mainstream'. While asserting its independence in designating the speaker, the Journal attempted to accommodate the views of the bank and the following year invited John Kenneth Gailbraith to deliver the lecture.

Gailbraith's lecture was one of the more memorable public lectures delivered at the LSE during the 1980s. It took place in the Old Theatre with members of the audience crammed into every available space and students literally sitting at Gailbraith's feet as he delivered his lecture. If anything, its effect on the audience from the bank was worse than Galtung the year before. Gailbraith delivered a scorching critique of Reaganomics and Thatcherism as the bank's representatives once again fidgeted nervously in their seats. The problem was that, whereas Galtung could be dismissed as a 'radical, left-wing crank', it was hard to get more mainstream and establishment than Gailbraith.

Ali Mazrui delivered the last of the lectures. As with the previous two lectures, it did not contain an argument that the representative of Chase Manhattan found easy to digest. Its five-year commitment over, the bank declined to renew the agreement to fund the lecture series.

Several aspects of *Millennium's* activities through this period are worth noting. Firstly, in terms of content there is not a great deal that sets the Journal apart from other journals at the time. Secondly, although there is a constant undercurrent of concerns with theoretical issues, a great deal of what the Journal publishes in this period might be broadly characterised as 'high journalism' or current affairs, with a predominance of FPA of individual countries or contemporary issues. Thirdly, and relatedly, is the degree to which *Millennium* was an active participant in what might now be characterised as the 'international public sphere'—the realm of decentralised, democratic, cosmopolitan discourse that provides the context for the articulation and discussion of social demands and our understanding of the 'political' and 'political community'. This has particularly been pursued via the conferences and public lectures the Journal has organised.

While the second of these trajectories—the current-affairs, FPA focus—would continue through the Journal's second decade,[13] in the following years the Journal would undergo a period of significant change in two areas: its commercial and financial well-being, and its academic content and theoretical orientation. Commercially and financially, from Vol. 10 the Journal entered into a three-year publishing arrangement with Martin Robertson. Although this was not renewed, the changes put in place during this period, along with the IT revolution and the rise of desktop publishing packages, would subsequently provide the Journal with the secure financial footing it had lacked up to that point.

Theory is Always . . .

When *Millennium* started its second decade, the political, economic, social and academic milieu was dramatically different from that in which it was established: revolutions had taken place in Nicaragua and Iran, the Soviet invasion of Afghanistan marked the start of the 'second' Cold War, and the 'New Right' had consolidated its political hold in the US and western Europe. Within IR, a number of important developments are discernible: regime theory arrives on the scene; normative theory, particularly concerning the ethics of war, emerges; nationalism comes into view; democratic peace theory is about to take off; and there are continuing explorations of interdependence, transnationalism and associated theoretical positions, along with the further articulation of structuralist/neo-Marxian positions. In the face of these alternative perspectives there are (re)statements and (re)assertions of political realism—including, most importantly, Hedley Bull's English School/Grotian account of international society and Kenneth Waltz's structural realism.[14]

In social and political theory, there are continuing discussions on epistemology, the character of modernity and the rise of postmodernism. There are important contributions from some of the central figures in contemporary continental political theory, as well as a rapidly growing secondary literature on them. In addition, the liberal-communitarian debate is unfolding, while feminism is consolidating as a major theoretical position.

In this context *Millennium* undergoes a transition that would see it move from being a journal concerned with both the theoretical and substantive content of competing paradigms to one that was located firmly within and making major contributions to some of the most important theoretical developments and debates within the discipline.[15] For better or worse, by the end of its second decade *Millennium* would be widely associated with the post-positivist, critical turn in international theory.[16]

Central to this development within the Journal and the wider discipline was the publication of Vol. 10 No. 2 in the summer of 1981. The importance of this issue is twofold: it is the first self-consciously 'theoretical' Special Issue and it contains Robert Cox's landmark piece, 'Social Forces, States and World Order: Beyond International Relations Theory'.[17] Published two years after Waltz's *Theory of International Politics* it was to become a central touchstone in the counter-discourse to the ontological and epistemological hegemony of the 'neo-neo consensus'.[18]

Cox's contribution set out a number of powerful positions that continue to echo in IR theoretical discourses: the distinction between 'problem-solving'

forms of theory and critical theory; the collapse of the
false distinction between theory and practice; the need for
historically nuanced accounts of how current social,
political, and economic practices came into being; a
normative impulse; and a praxeological concern.[19] All of
these would come to be central characteristics of various
forms of critical international theory.[20] All of these were
summed up in Cox's now famous aphorism, 'theory is
always for someone or for some purpose'. While not
necessarily novel or earth shattering in the wider realm of
social and political theory, such was the insular and
cocooned nature of IR theory at the time that his
interventions were like thunderbolts.

Both within the discipline and in the Journal, the
opening salvos of critical international theory did not
produce an immediate deluge of similar interventions.[21] It
would be another six years before the Journal returned to
these concerns in a sustained fashion: first in the form of
contributions in and responses to the Special Issue on
'The Study of International Relations' in Vol. 16,[22]
particularly the claim that 'critical theory represented the
next stage in international theory',[23] and more
concertedly with the Vol. 17 which was remarkable for its
theoretical content across all three issues and in particular
the dual contributions in the opening toward post-
structural/postmodern theorising and bringing gender to
the fore in international theory.

The contributions in Vol. 17 No. 2 mark the full turn of
the Journal on a post-positivist theoretical course that
would make it the site of several important theoretical
interventions in the discipline.[24] In particular, the
'Introduction' on philosophical traditions by James Der
Derian, Nick Rengger's re-reading of classical
international theory and Richard Ashley's 'double
reading' of Bull's *Anarchical Society* all provide clear
examples of the kinds of intrusions and disruptions that
were to follow in the wake of drawing on/in post-
structuralist/postmodernist theory. The agenda was

clear: to subvert dominant networks of representation through a process of deconstructing the hierarchical privileging of concepts and practices within world politics in order to create the space in which the 'other' could speak and act. The aim was no less than to reinscribe theory/practice in global politics.

The second major theoretical intervention in international theory and the agenda of the discipline came in the form of the second Special Issue in Vol. 17 on 'Women and International Relations'.[25] It is now difficult to imagine, but at the time this was the first sustained discussion of these issues in IR.[26] Pointedly noting the absence of such concerns from the wider discipline, evident even in their absence from the three previous theory Special Issues of *Millennium*, the contributions to Vol. 17 No. 3 forcefully drove home the extent to which international theory and practices were not gender neutral but deeply embedded with gendered constructs. Sharing the epistemological and ontological concerns of other forms of critical international theory, the contributions demonstrated the manner in which the division between the 'public' and the 'private' played themselves out in the practices of world politics, particularly in the realm of development. Explicit or implicit in these interventions is a concern with marginalisation and social exclusion, and the dissolution of the dominant theoretical and institutional edifices.

The Special Issue was followed up in Vol. 18 No. 2 with a 'discussion section' on 'Women and International Relations'. This included a piece by Robert Keohane in which he attempted to rationalise the contribution of some (but not all) forms of feminist theory[27]—which in turn promoted a scathing response from Cynthia Weber highlighting how Keohane's piece encapsulated all the 'normalising' strategies that radical forms of feminist theory were attempting to unmask and overturn.[28]

Theoretical concerns would continue to manifest themselves in *Millennium* over the next three

volumes—including pieces on relativism and ethics, re-
reading classical (international) political theory, feminism
and peace studies, the causes of war debate,
postmodernism and international theory, historical
sociological takes on the state and violence, the English
School and the 'good life', and Gramscian IPE. Some of
these contributions could be located within a broadly
post-positivist agenda. However, the majority of the
pieces in the Journal explored both mainstream and new
agendas from fairly traditional perspectives. The inverse
would be the case in the Journal's third decade.

Millennium: Journal of *Critical* International Studies?

As was the case with the founding of the Journal and the
start of its second decade, the opening of *Millennium*'s
third decade coincides with dramatic changes in world
politics: the fall of the Berlin Wall, the end of the Cold
War and the implosion of the Soviet Union and its
associated alliance structure; Iraq's invasion of Kuwait;
pro-democracy demonstrations in Tianamen Square; and
the end of apartheid in South Africa. Over the horizon
were a string of complex humanitarian emergencies and
genocide in Rwanda.

Within the discipline, there were two competing
trends: one was intellectual closure; the other was a
continued orientation towards intellectual and theoretical
pluralism, generating new positions and perspectives,
often in reaction to the aspect of closure. The aspect of
closure was exemplified in the 'debate' between
neorealism and neoliberalism, and in particular their
differing views on explaining the nature of cooperation,
and eventually coalescing into the 'neo-neo' consensus.
Not unconnected to the neoliberal agenda was the
consolidation of IPE as a major aspect of the study of
international relations.

Aspects of theoretical pluralism and innovation were connected with previous ongoing debates inside and outside the discipline, as well as thinking through the meaning and impact of the end of the Cold War. Among these developments were: the agent-structure debate which would eventually transmogrify into constructivist theories of IR; the rise of normative theory and the arrival of the cosmopolitan-communitarian debate; further articulations of the English School and the appellation of 'international political theory'; the debates over the 'end of history', the democratic peace, and the 'clash of civilisations'; and the beginnings of what would eventually be cast as issues of 'global governance'. The period was also characterised by sustained statements in further developing forms of critical and postmodern international theory, as well as feminist international theory.

Within social and political theory there were ongoing discussions about the nature and character of modernity and the postmodern, as well as major contributions to the ongoing development of feminist political theory. An outgrowth of these developments was discussions and debates surrounding notions of identity, politics and the political, and (nonfoundational) ethics.

Within this post-Cold War political and academic environment, *Millennium* entered a period of sustained theoretical engagement and established itself as one of the most important voices in international theory, publishing challenging and innovative contributions that articulate alternative, sometimes dissonant, theoretical perspectives and explore subject areas with which IR has had little or no serious engagement.[29] For all intents and purposes, *Millennium's* self-identity consolidates into a journal of post-positivist or critical international studies.

The critical orientation of the Journal—and the broad understanding of what this entails—is evident in the contributions published in this period. Three aspects of the Journal's work bring this into sharper focus: the content of the Special Issues; the dialogues on critical thematics that have taken place within and across different issues (and even volumes) of the Journal; and the thematic focus of the books that have come out of its conferences and Special Issues. Alongside the main articles, these have especially made an impact on the agenda of IR theory, often anticipating new trends and challenging old paths of research.

Special Issues

Since Vol. 20, 13 Special Issues have been published containing a rich array of diverse topics, themes and theoretical perspectives. These are

Reimagining the Nation (Vol. 20, No. 3, 1991)[30]
Beyond International Society (Vol. 21, No. 2, 1992)[31]
Culture in International Relations (Vol. 22, No. 3, 1993)[32]
Social Movements and World Politics (Vol. 22, No. 3, 1994)[33]
The Globalisation of Liberalism (Vol. 24, No. 3, 1995)[34]
Poverty in World Politics: Whose Global Era? (Vol. 25, No. 3, 1996)[35]
War Endings: Reasons, Strategies and Implications (Vol. 26, No. 3, 1997)[36]
Ethics and International Relations (Vol. 27, No. 3, 1998)[37]
Gendering 'the International' (Vol. 27, No. 4, 1998)[38]
Territoriality, Identity and Movement in International Relations (Vol. 28, No. 3, 1999)
Religion and International Relations (Vol. 29, No. 3, 2000)[39]
Images and Narratives in World Politics (Vol. 30, No. 3, 2001)[40]
Pragmatism in International Relations Theory (Vol. 31, No. 3, 2002).

Through a reading of the contributions to the Special Issues, as well as those in other issues of the Journal, a number of themes stand out. These give an indication of the range of theoretical issues, concerns, questions, concepts and approaches associated with the post-positivist turn in international theory that have been articulated, addressed and developed within the pages of *Millennium.*

The first of these is the re-examination and radical re-working of the mainstream agenda and lexicon of the territorialised, sovereign nation-state and the dominant discourse and practices that underpin it, including the interrogation of discipline defining concepts such as 'anarchy' and 'international society'. Of particular interest is an exploration of how the dominant discourses of IR are constructed, maintained, resisted or eroded. Linked to this is the excavation of the epistemological and ontological assumptions underlying these and alternative discourses.

The second theme is an engagement with discourses of identity, the problem of subjectivities, and the construction of self/other distinctions. Closely linked to this is the concern with the thematic of borders, territoriality and order as well as the associated dynamics, politics and ethics of inclusion and exclusion. This, in turn, links into explorations of our changing understandings of gender, culture, and religion.

Thirdly, there is an interest in exploring the possibilities of ameliorative epistemology, of *poiesis*, and of 'imaginative (re)construction' as the basis for theoretical, practical and ethical ways of engaging with and managing difference in a world of value pluralism. This manifests itself in the explorations of possibilities for plural allegiances, for non-territorial expressions of identity, the deterritorialisation of politics, and the development of a post-Westphalian political order. Closely linked to this is an interest in exploring the strategies by which this might be pursued, ranging from the use of aesthetics to the potentially transformative role of particular social and political agents such as social movements, to the prospects for cross-civilisational dialogues, to the articulation and invocation of non-foundational ethics.

Dialogues

Millennium's critical orientation and its commitment to dialogue is further evident in some of the exchanges that have ensued within and across its pages. These have sometimes been encouraged (if not engineered) by editors; sometimes they have developed in a more spontaneous and organic fashion as a consequence of submissions in response to a piece already published.

An example of these dialogues can be seen in the exchange on the nature and tasks of critical international theory[41] as well as in the exchange initiated by Justin Rosenberg on 'classical social analysis' and the 'international imagination'.[42] Other examples would be the exchange between David Campbell and Daniel Warner on Emmanuel Lévinas and non-foundational ethics in international relations;[43] between Christian Heine and Benno Teschke and their critics on historical materialism, dialectic and international theory;[44] between Martin van Creveld and his critics on 'feminising the military';[45] between Fred Dallmayr and his respondents on the nature and possibility of a 'global conversation';[46] and the discussion of Hardt and Negri's path-breaking book, *Empire*.[47]

Conference Volumes

A third manifestation of *Millennium*'s critical orientation and commitment to debate can be found in its freestanding conference volumes, and in particular those which resulted from its 25th anniversary celebrations in 1996. As part of these celebrations, *Millennium* organised a two-and-a-half day conference. Presenters and participants were invited on the basis primarily of some sort of connection with the Journal over the two-plus decades: either as a former member of the editorial teams or as a contributor. Panels were organised on the basis of the papers that were offered in a way that attempted to make some sense of the diversity of topics. In the aftermath of the conference, it became evident that it was possible to group many, though by no means all, of the conference papers under three broad themes that again reflected core concerns of post-positivist international theory: an interrogation of our understanding of the political,[48] an engagement with the possibility of movement beyond the cosmopolitan-communitarian divide in international ethics,[49] and an examination of our understanding of the state and identities in late modernity.[50]

Conclusion: *Millennium*, the Political and the 'International Public Sphere'

What are the implications and consequences of *Millennium's* evolution over a 30-year period? Where does it leave us in terms of the initial vision of Fred Northedge and his group of students back in February 1971? In many ways, the journey travelled through the pages of the Journal has been true to the initial ethos of that group of individuals. *Millennium* has been, and continues to be, a place of intellectual pluralism and diversity, a site of dialogue where new ideas are developed, a safe haven for those seeking to articulate positions, orientations and perspectives that are at odds with the dominant discourses in the discipline. It still provides a place in which contributions from research students will rub shoulders with the great and the good of the discipline. And, at least at the level of student subscriptions, it is still financially accessible.

One consequence of maintaining its underlying ethos has been its non-participation in some of the mainstream theoretical orientations and debates within the discipline. For example, it has made very little contribution to the neorealist-neoliberal debate. Given its own 'reflectivist' theoretical agenda this is hardly surprising and probably no great loss to either the 'neo-neo debate' or the Journal. More surprisingly, it has made only limited direct contributions to the development of constructivism in international theory, with the exception of Friedrich Kratochwil's notable review of Alexander Wendt's *Social Theory of International Politics*.[51] This is to the Journal's detriment, and possibly due to the neo-neo infused direction that the major approach to constructivism ended up adopting.

A major implication is connected to the arguments Rosenberg develops in his 'classic social analysis' article. This is the charge that in the move to a primary engagement with theory, and in particular post-positivist theory, *Millennium* has lost touch with the substantive, the political, the praxeological. Stuck in the nether reaches of meta-theory it has become abstract and detached from the 'real stuff of international relations'. Curiously, this is a charge that is levelled at it both from the more traditional, mainstream members of the discipline (and the Department) who think the Journal is uninterested in serious empirical research, and from the Marxian-informed left who support the call for a critical international theory but bemoan the lack of identifiable social agents of change and transformation.[52]

There are three responses that can be made to this. The first is to note that this overplays the theory/practice divide within the Journal. While it is the case that the overwhelming majority of pieces published in the first fifteen volumes were policy-oriented in nature and embraced an orientation that saw theory and practice as two distinct domains, a considerable majority of these addressed and articulated theoretical concerns or questions that were explored via a substantive issue.

Second, although the overwhelming majority of contributions in the last dozen volumes have been theoretical in orientation they have not been without substantive content or practical political concerns—even by those authors adopting more pronounced post-structuralists positions. An incomplete list of such concerns would include: the implosion of Yugoslavia, the politics of the Middle East, security in post-Cold War Europe, environmental issues, diplomacy, peacekeeping, the role of non-governmental organisations, humanitarian intervention, globalisation, and global civil society.

The third, and most important, response takes us straight back to Vol. 10 No. 2 and the article by Robert Cox that helped consolidate *Millennium*'s evolution and self-identity: the argument that the distinction between theory and practice is itself a false dichotomy. To this extent, then, there is no link between theory and practice that somehow needs to be recovered or re-animated from the early years of the Journal, but a recognition that theory is itself a form of practice, a substantive act, a political act in the deepest understanding of what 'the political' entails. This does not deny that the praxeological questions regarding the agents of social change and transformation are important; it is to recognise that they are difficult and not so straightforward as they may have appeared to be in the past. In providing a pluralistic space for these critical endeavours *Millennium* has made and continues to make a real, serious and genuine contribution to the 'international public sphere'—and long may it continue to do so with the enthusiasm, verve, innovation and panache it has shown over the last 31 years.

References

1. This is not to deny that there were and are important exceptions to this overall characterisation. Nor is it meant to imply that the contributions made from within this theoretical orientation are without merit. Indeed, for a considerable period of time in the history of IR theory, it provided one of the most important counter-discourses to North American behaviourally infused Realism.

2. Alfred Lord Tennyson, 'The Two Voices' [www.tennysonpoetry.hom.att.net] (20 October 2002).

3. He was given the title of Associate Editor. This has been accorded to each subsequent Convenor of the Department. From Vol. 10 it was also given to one of the outgoing editors as a way of ensuring smooth editorial transitions and easy access to 'institutional memory'.

4. Typically, the editorial board is mostly composed of students on one-year taught postgraduate degrees, as well as doctoral research students and, in the early days, a smattering of undergraduates.

5. There have been occasions when these democratic processes have taken the form of affirming a single set of candidates for the post who more often than not were cajoled into editing the Journal over several sustained sessions in the Beaver's Retreat bar at the LSE. Since Vol. 11, the two editors have been research students. Interestingly, through the mid-1980s, editing *Millennium* was seen as detrimental to the process of completing one's PhD. Indeed, it was widely viewed by some departmental staff as a kind of black hole. However, from roughly Vol. 14 onward, the

completion rate amongst editors of the Journal has been very high and, more importantly, many have moved on into academic positions within the discipline. Yet, as the fees for pursuing research studies escalated, a number of possible editorial candidates came to the conclusion that they simply could not afford to edit the Journal.

6. Incoming editors, particularly those from North America, would have to learn that 'Millennium' was spelt with two 'n's' and be rapidly socialised into the Journal's editorial and stylistic nuances. In the early days there were also endless editorial debates on single vs. double quotation marks (eventually being resolved by moving to just single quotation marks), the hyphenation or not of words such as cooperation, coordination, long term, decision making, etc.

7. The growing subscriptions helped to provide the finances necessary to publish the Journal. But, adhering to Northedge's principle that the Journal be affordable, the low cover price was not sufficient to cover all costs. In its first ten years, the Department and the LSE carried much of the real costs of the producing the Journal directly and indirectly. In addition, the Journal had successfully garnered outside financial support from the Leverhulme Foundation that ran for a five-year period. But with escalating printing costs, the Journal was moving inexorably towards a serious financial crisis.

8. James Rosenau, 'International Studies in a Transnational World', *Millennium: Journal of International Studies* 5, no. 1 (1976): 1-20 and F.S. Northedge, 'Transnationalism: The American Illusion', *Millennium: Journal of International Studies* 5, no. 1 (1976): 21-27. It is interesting to re-read this exchange in light of contemporary debates regarding 'globalisation'.

9. A Special Issue was not an additional issue of the journal in any particular volume but an issue within a volume that had a thematic coherence. From Vol. 9 onwards, there would be a Special Issue (sometimes two, even occasionally as a genuine fourth issue) in each volume. These would become important vehicles for editors to pursue topics close to their own research interest. They also became the medium through which the Journal would make some of its most important interventions in and contributions to ongoing debates in international theory.

10. The last of these included a paper delivered by the then rising academic star, later Director of the LSE, Anthony Giddens on 'Foucault, Violence and the Nation-state' (paper presented at the *Millennium* Conference on 'Contemporary Social Theory and the Problem of War and Peace', 18 October 1985, London).

11. See Lawrence Hagen, ed., *The Crisis in Western Security* (London: Croom Helm, 1982); Diana Tuzzi, ed., *Latin America in the World Economy* (London: Gower, 1983); and Mark Schaffer, ed., *Technology Transfer and East-West Relations* (London: Croom Helm, 1985).

12. See, Ernst Gellner, 'Patterns of Dissidence', *Millennium: Journal of International Studies* 6, no. 1 (1977): 73-80; Raymond Aron, 'War and Industrial Society: A Reappraisal', *Millennium: Journal of International Studies* 7, no. 3 (1978): 78-80; Johan Galtung, 'A Structural Theory of Imperialism—Ten Years Later', *Millennium: Journal of International Studies* 9, no. 3 (1980): 181-96; John Kenneth Galbraith, 'The Social Consensus and the Conservative Onslaught', *Millennium: Journal of International Studies* 11, no. 1 (1982): 1-13; and Ali A. Mazrui, 'Africa: The Political Culture of Nationhood and the Political

Economy of State', *Millennium: Journal of International Studies* 12, no. 3 (1983): 201-10.

13. Notably in the form of the special issues on the Falklands crisis, *Millennium: Journal of International Studies* 12, no. 1 (1982); Central America, *Millennium: Journal of International Studies* 13, no. 2 (1984), Nationalism, *Millennium: Journal of International Studies* 14, no. 2 (1985); arms control, *Millennium: Journal of International Studies* 15, no. 2 (1986); Japan, *Millennium: Journal of International Studies* 18, no. 3 (1989); the environment, *Millennium: Journal of International Studies* 19, no. 3 (1990); and the 'Special Section' on MNCs and sovereignty, *Millennium: Journal of International Studies* 20, no. 2 (1991).

14. See respectively, Hedley Bull, *The Anarchical Society: A Study of Order in World Politics* (London: Macmillan, 1977) and Kenneth Waltz, *Theory of International Politics* (Reading, MA: Addison Wesley, 1979).

15. On a very rough count, in the first decade of the Journal less than 20 per cent of the articles were self-consciously about 'theory'. In the following ten-year period this would double to about 40 per cent. By the third decade almost 70 per cent of all articles published would be 'theory' articles.

16. It was also during this period that *Millennium* fostered its first and only band: 'Dr J and the MPhils'. Over a one-and-a-half year period they played at several parties jointly organised by the Journal and the Department performing specially re-written cover versions of songs by, among others, David Bowie, Elvis Costello and the Talking Heads. As is so often the case, the band fell apart as its members went in different directions. The vocalist, Dr J returned to the States working in the financial sector in New York while writing airport novels, science fiction and eventually an on-line magazine; the lead guitarist

became a professor of economics specialising in transition economies; the rhythm guitarist became caught up in making contentious claims about the future directions of international theory.

17. Robert Cox, 'Social Forces, States and World Order: Beyond International Relations Theory', *Millennium: Journal of International Studies* 10, no. 2 (1981): 126-55. What is not widely known is that the publication of Cox's piece was not a foregone conclusion. It strongly divided the then editorial team with some members of the team wishing to reject it outright. It took three separate editorial board meetings to reach a consensus in favour of publication. Such was the turmoil and uncertainty created by this that in its aftermath it was agreed that contributions to future Special Issues would continue to be externally refereed, but the editorial decisions regarding which contributions to publish would not be put to the vicissitudes of the democratic processes of the editorial board, but be in the hands of editors, deputy editors and associate editors of the day.

18. It is important to note that at roughly the same time, three other theoretical interventions were also made that contributed to the developing post-positivist turn in IR theory. They were: Richard Ashley, 'Political Realism and Human Interests', *International Studies Quarterly* 25, no. 2 (1981): 221-26; R.B.J Walker, 'Political Theory and the Transformation of World Politics', *World Order Studies Program*, Occasional Paper no. 8 (Princeton, NJ: Centre for International Studies, 1980); and Andrew Linklater, *Men and Citizens in International Theory* (London: Macmillan, 1981).

19. See also J. Maclean, 'Political Theory, International Theory and Problems of Ideology', *Millennium: Journal of International Studies* 10, no. 2 (1981): 102-25.

20. The term 'critical international theory' is used here, and elsewhere in the article, in its widest possible meaning (i.e., not delimited to Habermasean-informed theory) and as synonymous with 'post-positivist international theory'.

21. Over the next five volumes of the Journal there would be theoretical contributions, for example on regime theory and normative theory, but none adopting a self-avowedly critical theory orientation. The overwhelming majority of the pieces in the Journal revert to type and cover a range of 'inter-paradigmatic' topics similar to those in the first ten volumes.

22. Special Issue, 'The Study of International Relations', *Millennium: Journal of International Studies* 16, no. 2 (1987). See also, Hugh Dyer and Leon Mangasarian, eds., *The Study of International Relations* (London: Macmillan, 1988).

23. Mark Hoffman, 'Critical Theory and the Inter-Paradigm Debate', *Millennium: Journal of International Studies* 16, no. 2 (1987): 231-49.

24. Special Issue, 'Philosophical Traditions in International Relations', *Millennium: Journal of International Studies* 17, no. 2 (1988). However, only the piece by Ashley adopts an avowedly post-structuralist orientation.

25. Special Issue, 'Women and International Relations', *Millennium: Journal of International Studies* 17, no. 3 (1988). It is worth noting that the title of the issue is neither 'feminism and international relation', nor 'gender and international relations' though a number of the pieces address both of these along with the category 'women'. Few, if any, of the pieces are located within 'feminist postmodernism'; most would be characterised as either feminist empiricist or feminist standpoint/feminist critical theory.

However, from this number onwards, the divergent strands of feminist international theory have been well-represented in the journal, including many from a 'feminist postmodern' perspective, including those in the follow-up 10th anniversary Special Issue 'Gendering "the International"', *Millennium: Journal of International Studies* 27, no. 4 (1998). An interesting characteristic of many of these contributions is the extent to which they are often linked directly to a concern with practical politics.

26. Needless to say, outside IR, women, feminism and gender had been an ongoing contribution to debates in social and political theory, as well as development studies, for the better part of a decade.

27. Robert O. Keohane, 'International Relations Theory: Contributions of a Feminist Standpoint', *Millennium: Journal of International Studies* 18, no. 2 (1989): 245-53.

28. Cynthia Weber, 'Good Girls, Little Girls and Bad Girls: Male Paranoia in Robert Keohane's Critique of Feminist International Relations', *Millennium: Journal of International Studies* 23, no. 2 (1994): 337-49.

29. The impetus to explore these new areas derives from the interests of each new editorial team and their own research agendas and views about what are the cutting edge topics in the discipline. For much of *Millennium*'s third decade, this was fostered and sustained by a series of PhD research workshops that ran for almost a six-year period within the Department of International Relations at the LSE. These included: an 'International Political Theory' workshop; a 'Postmodernism and International Relations' workshop; a 'Critical International Theory' workshop; a 'Modernity and International Relations' workshop; and a 'Historical Materialism' workshop. There were also workshops that lasted just a year in length, including one on 'Gender and Critical Theory'

and another on 'Pragmatism and International Theory'.

30. See also Adam Lerner and Marjorie Ringrose, eds., *Reimagining the Nation* (London: Open University Press, 1993).

31. See also Rick Fawn and Jeremy Larkins, eds., *International Society after the Cold War: Anarchy and Order Reconsidered* (London: Macmillan, 1996).

32. See also Dominique Jacquin-Berdal, Andrew Oros and Marco Verweij, eds., *Culture in World Politics* (New York: St. Martin's Press, 1998).

33. Sadly, this particular issue was never revised for book publication.

34. See also Eivind Hovden and Edward Keene, eds., *The Globalisation of Liberalism* (London: Palgarve, 2002).

35. See Sarah Owen-Vandersluis and Paris Yeros, eds., *Poverty in World Politics: Whose Global Era?* (London: Macmillan, 1999).

36. Many though not all of the contributions in this issue would make this Special Issue the least post-positivist in orientation.

37. See also Hakan Seckinelgin and Hideaki Shinoda, eds., *Ethics and International Relations* (London: Palgrave, 2001).

38. See also Louiza Odysseos and Hakan Seckinelgin, eds., *Gendering the International* (London: Palgrave, 2002).

39. See also Fabio Petito and Pavlos Hatzopoulos, eds., *Religion in International Relations: The Return From Exile* (London: Palgrave, 2003).

40. This issue is unique in that it includes, for only the second time in the pages of the Journal, the use of a full colour reproduction of works of art, with paintings by Turner, Towmbly and Bourgeois included in Christine Sylvester's discussion of the role of aesthetics in international relations. The first

was a full colour reprint of Holbien's painting, 'The Ambassador' in Costas Constantinou, 'Diplomatic Representations . . . or Who Framed the Ambassadors', *Millennium: Journal of International Studies* 23, no. 1 (1994): 1-24.

41. Hoffman, 'Critical Theory'; Nicholas J. Rengger, 'Going Critical: A Response to Hoffman', *Millennium: Journal of International Studies* 17, no. 1 (1988): 81-90; Mark Hoffman, 'Conversations on Critical International Relations Theory', *Millennium: Journal of International Studies* 17, no. 1 (1988): 91-96; Andrew Linklater, 'The Question of the Next Stage in International Relations Theory: A Critical-Theoretical Point of View', *Millennium: Journal of International Studies* 21, no. 1 (1992): 77-98; Mark Neufeld, 'Reflexivity and International Relations Theory', *Millennium: Journal of International Relations* 22, no. 1 (1993): 53-76; Chris Brown, '"Turtles All the Way Down": Anti-Foundationalism, Critical Theory and International Relations', *Millennium: Journal of International Studies* 23, no. 2 (1994): 213-36; Jürgen Haacke, 'Theory and Praxis in International Relations: Habermas, Self-Reflection, Rational Argumentation', *Millennium: Journal of International Studies* 25, no. 2 (1996): 255-90.

42. Justin Rosenberg, 'The International Imagination: IR and "Classical Social Analysis"', *Millennium: Journal of International Studies* 23, no. 1 (1994): 85-108; Mervyn Frost, 'The Role of Normative Theory', *Millennium: Journal of International Studies* 23, no. 1 (1994): 109-18; Chris Boyle, 'Imagining the World Market: IPE and the Task of Social Theory', *Millennium: Journal of International Studies* 23, no. 2 (1994): 351-64; David Campbell, 'Political Excess and the Limits of Imagination', *Millennium: Journal of International Relations* 23, no. 2 (1994): 365-76; Fred Halliday,

'Theory and Ethics in International Relations: The Contradictions of C. Wright Mills', *Millennium: Journal of International Studies* 23, no. 2 (1994): 377-86; Mark Neufeld, 'Who's Afraid of Meta-Theory?', *Millennium: Journal of International Studies* 23, no. 2 (1994): 387-94; and Steve Smith, 'Rearranging the Deckchairs on the Ship Called Modernity: Rosenberg, Epistemology and Emancipation', *Millennium: Journal of International Studies* 23, no. 2 (1994): 395-405.

43. Daniel Warner, 'Levinas, Buber and the Concept of Otherness in International Relations: A Reply to David Campbell', *Millennium: Journal of International Studies* 25, no. 1 (1996): 111-28 and David Campbell, 'The Politics of Radical Interdependence: A Rejoinder to Daniel Warner', *Millennium: Journal of International Studies* 25, no.1 (1996): 129-41.

44. Christian Heine and Benno Teschke, 'Sleeping Beauty and the Dialectical Awakening: On the Potential of Dialectic for International Relations', *Millennium: Journal of International Studies* 25, no. 2 (1996): 399-424; Mathias Albert and Yosef Lapid, 'On Dialectic and IR Theory: Hazards of a Proposed Marriage', *Millennium: Journal of International Studies* 26, no. 2 (1997): 403-15; Hayo Krombach, 'Dialectic as the Philosophical Science of Socio-Historical Relations', *Millennium: Journal of International Studies* 26, no. 2 (1997): 417-36; Friedrich Kratochwil, 'Awakening or Somnambulation', *Millennium: Journal of International Studies* 26, no. 2 (1997): 437-42; Ekkehart Krippendorff, 'Be Your Own Prince', *Millennium: Journal of International Studies* 26, no. 2 (1997): 443-47; Mark Neufeld, 'The "Dialectical Awakening" in International Relations: For and Against', *Millennium: Journal of International Studies* 26, no. 2 (1997): 449-54; and Christian Heine and Benno Teschke, 'On Dialectic and International Relations: A Reply to Our

Critics', *Millennium: Journal of International Studies* 26, no. 2 (1997): 455-70.

45. Martin van Creveld, 'The Great Illusion: Women in the Military', *Millennium: Journal of International Studies* 29, no. 2 (2000): 429-42; Jean Bethke Elshtain, '"Shooting" at the Wrong Target: A Response to van Creveld', *Millennium: Journal of International Studies* 29, no. 2 (2000): 443-48; and Christopher Coker, 'Humanising Warfare, or Why van Creveld May Be Missing the "Big Picture"', *Millennium: Journal of International Studies* 29, no. 2 (2000): 449-60.

46. Fred Dallmayr, 'Conversation Across Boundaries: Political Theory and Global Diversity', *Millennium: Journal of International Studies* 30, no. 2 (2001): 331-47; William E. Connolly, 'Cross-State Citizen Networks: A Response to Dallmayr', *Millennium: Journal of International Studies* 30, no. 2 (2001): 349-55; Nicholas Rengger, 'The Boundaries of Conversation: A Response to Dallmayr', *Millennium: Journal of International Relations* 30, no. 2 (2001): 357-64.

47. Tarak Barkawai and Mark Laffey, 'Retrieving the Imperial: *Empire* and International Relations', *Millennium: Journal of International Relations* 31, no. 1 (2002): 109-27; Alex Callinicos, 'The Actuality of Imperialism', *Millennium: Journal of International Studies* 31, no. 2 (2002): 319-26; Martin Shaw, 'Post-Imperial and Quasi-Imperial: State and Empire in a Global Era', *Millennium: Journal of International Relations* 31, no. 2 (2002): 327-36; and R.B.J. Walker, 'On the Immanence/Imminence of Empire', *Millennium: Journal of International Relations* 31, no. 2 (2002): 337-45.

48. Michi Ebata and Beverly Neufeld, eds., *Confronting the Political in International Relations* (London: Macmillan, 2000).

49. Marina Lensu and Jan-Stefan Fritz, eds., *Value Pluralism, Normative Theory and International Relations* (London: Macmillan, 1999).
50. Sarah Owen–Vandersluis, ed., *The State and Identity Construction in International Relations* (London: Macmillan, 2000).
51. Friedrich Kratochwil, 'Constructing a New Orthodoxy? Wendt's "Social Theory of International Relations" and the Constructivist Challenge', *Millennium: Journal of International Studies* 29, no. 1 (2000): 73-102.
52. See, for example, Alejandro Colas, 'The Politics of *Millennium:* Theory and Practice in a Critical Journal' (paper presented at the *Millennium* 25th Anniversary Conference, 17-19 October 1996, London).

Millennium Editors

For more than thirty years postgraduates in the Department have succeeded to the Editorship of *Millennium: Journal of International Studies.* This list is intended not only as a tribute to those whose commitment and enthusiasm have made this Journal the leading academic publication in IR to be entirely student-run, but also as an attempt to trace the different paths followed by such a community of people after their memorable experience at *Millennium.* Space only forbids that we acknowledge all members of the Editorial Boards and Editorial Teams who over the years have proved an equally indispensable force in the development of the Journal. Many thanks to all those who have helped in the compilation of this list, and apologies to those whose current affiliation could not be successfully retrieved.

Volume 31 (2002)

Harry Bauer
PhD student, Department of International Relations, LSE
Elisabetta Brighi
PhD student, Department of International Relations, LSE

Volume 30 (2001)

Chris Berzins (no. 2 and 3)
PhD student, Department of International Relations, LSE
Armida De la Garza (no.1)
PhD student, Department of International Relations, LSE
Helen Kambouri
PhD student, Department of International Relations, LSE

Volume 29 (2000)

Pavlos Hatzopoulos
PhD student, Department of International Relations, LSE
Fabio Petito
Visiting Assistant Professor, Ecole Supérieure de Commerce de Paris and Lecturer, Istituto Universitario Orientale, Napoli, Italy

Volume 28 (1999)

Jason Ackleson
Assistant Professor, Department of Government and Associate Director, University Honors Program, New Mexico State University
Nicola Short
Lecturer, Department of Political Science, York University, Canada

Volume 27 (1998)

Louiza Odysseos (no. 4)
Lecturer, Department of Political Studies, School of Oriental and African Studies, London
Hakan Seckinelgin
Lecturer, Social Policy Department, LSE
Hideaki Shinoda
Research Fellow, Institute for Peace Science, Hiroshima University, Japan

Volume 26 (1997)

Sanja Carolina
PhD Student, Department of International Relations, LSE
Per Hammarlund

Volume 25 (1996)

Sarah Owen-Vandersluis
Finance Manager, Ford Motor Company, London
Paris Yeros
Visiting Professor, Department of Economics, Federal University of Paraná, Brazil

Volume 24 (1995)

Eivind Hovden
> *Advisor, The Research Council of Norway, Oslo, Norway*

Edward Keene
> *Assistant Professor, The Sam Nunn School of International Affairs, Georgia Institute of Technology, Atlanta*

Volume 23 (1994)

Mairi Johnson
> *Executive Director, Research Department, Goldman Sachs, London*

Bice Maiguashca
> *Lecturer, School of Historical, Political and Sociological Studies, University of Exeter, England*

Volume 22 (1993)

Dominique Jacquin-Berdal
> *Lecturer, Department of International Relations, LSE*

Andrew Oros
> *Assistant Professor of Political Science and International Studies, Washington College, Maryland*

Marco Verweij
> *Associate Professor of Political Science, Singapore Management University*

Volume 21 (1992)

Jeremy Larkins
> *Occasional Teacher, Department of International Relations, LSE*

Rick Fawn (no. 2 and 3)
> *Senior Lecturer in International Relations, University of St. Andrews, Scotland*

Robert Newman

178

Volume 20 (1991)
Marjorie Martin-Ringrose

Evan Potter
Assistant Professor, Department of Communication, University of Ottawa, Canada

Volume 19 (1990)
Malory Greene
· *Acting Head of the Russia, NIS and South Eastern Europe Programmes, OECD, Paris*
Ian Rowlands
Associate Professor of Environment and Resource Studies, University of Waterloo, Ontario, Canada

Volume 18 (1989)
Charles Armstrong
Associate Professor of History and International Affairs, Columbia University, New York
Kathleen Newland
Co-Director, Migration Policy Institute, Washington DC

Volume 17 (1988)
Rebecca Grant
President, IRIS Independent Research, Washington DC
David Long
Associate Professor, The Norman Paterson School of International Affairs, Carleton University, Ottawa, Canada

Volume 16 (1987)
Hugh C. Dyer
Senior Lecturer in International Studies, The University of Leeds
Leon Mangasarian
German and International Affairs Correspondent, Deutsche Presse Agentur, Berlin, Germany

Volume 15 (1986)

J. Kurt Barling
Journalist and Broadcaster—Special Correspondent, BBC London News, London
Spyros Economides
Lecturer, Department of International Relations, LSE

Volume 14 (1985)

Panagiotis Bayz
Attorney, Morrison and Foerster LLP, Washington DC
Scheherazade Daneshkhu
Correspondent, Financial Times, London

Volume 13 (1984)

Mark E. Schaffer
Professor, Centre for Economic Reform and Transformation, Department of Economics, Heriot-Watt University, Edinburgh

Volume 12 (1983)

Carla Garapedian
Producer and Director, Channel 4 Dispatches, London
Jeffrey D. Myhre (no. 2 and 3)
Founding Editor, The Kensington Review, New York

Volume 11 (1982)

Ryszarda Biernat
Managing Director, Interlink Travel Agency, London
Daniel C. Goldwater
Managing Director, Goldman Sachs International, London

Volume 10 (1981)

Mark J. Hoffman
Lecturer, Department of International Relations and Dean of Undergraduate Studies, LSE
Paul J. Starobin (no. 1 and 2)
Staff Correspondent, The National Journal and Contributing Editor, The Atlantic Monthly, Washington DC

Volume 9 (1980)

Jane Sargent

Joyce Colwill

Volume 8 (1979)

Jana E. Bennett
Director of Television, BBC, London and Governor of LSE
Ann Rolfe-Kinder
Teacher, Connexions Programme, UK South-Central Region

Volume 7 (1978)

John E. Barrett
*Head, Policy Planning Section, Political Affairs Division,
NATO, Brussels*
Andrew P. Smith

Volume 6 (1977)

Ken Matthews
Principal Lecturer, Coventry Business School

Volume 5 (1976)

Richard Holdsworth (no. 1 and 2)
*Head of Information Technology in the Research Service of
the European Parliament, Luxembourg, and Researcher at
Egenis, the Economic and Social Research Council Centre for
Genomics in Society, University of Exeter, England*

Volume 4 (1975)

D.C. Liddel (no. 1 and 2)

Barbara Allen Roberson (no. 2 and 3)
*Lecturer, Department of Politics and International Studies,
Warwick University, England*

Volume 3 (1974)

Colin Hollis
   Former Federal Labour MP, Throsby, Australia

Volume 2 (1973)

Jeffrey Golden (no. 2 and 3)
   Partner and Co-Head of the US Law Group, Allen & Overy,
   London
Ken Kinney (no. 1)

Volume 1 (1971-72)

Barry Buzan (no. 3)
   Professor, Department of International Relations, LSE
Chris Stevens (no. 1 and 2)
   Research Fellow, Institute of Development Studies,
   University of Sussex, England

Index